BRINGING
ITALY
HOME

URSULA FERRIGNO

BRINGING ITALY HOME

PHOTOGRAPHY BY JASON LOWE

MITCHELL BEAZLEY

DEDICATION
To Daddy

BRINGING ITALY HOME
by Ursula Ferrigno

First published in Great Britain in 2001
by Mitchell Beazley, an imprint of
Octopus Publishing Group Ltd
2–4 Heron Quays, London E14 4JP
Reprinted 2002
This paperback edition first published in 2005

ISBN 1 84000 921 7

A CIP catalogue record for this book is available
from the British Library. The author and publisher
will be grateful for any information that will assist
them in keeping future editions up to date. Although
all reasonable care has been taken in the preparation
of this book, neither the publisher nor the author
can accept liability for any consequences arising
from the use thereof, or from the information
contained therein.

Commissioning Editor: Rebecca Spry
Art Director: Geoff Borin
Managing Editor: Jamie Grafton
Editor: Susan Fleming
Proof-reading: Maggie Pannell
Production: Nancy Roberts and Alex Wiltshire
Index: John Noble

Typeset in Minion and Trajan

Printed and bound by Toppan Printing Company
in China.

NOTE
All eggs are organic, free-range and the largest you can
find. Organic vegetables are best too.

CONTENTS

introduction 7

PRIMAVERA

spring **12**

ESTATE

summer **60**

AUTUNNO

autumn **126**

INVERNO

winter **182**

index **222**   acknowledgements **224**

INTRODUCTION

Italy captures your heart and binds you in a spell. Few people return from Italy without lasting memories of its lush countryside, vibrant cities and clear blue sky and sea. The food reflects this ever-changing landscape, with dishes that echo the sea, sky, country and city. This elusive magic is something that I wanted to distil in *Bringing Italy Home*.

The true food of Italy is found in villages, where little has changed over the centuries. Food is the whole focus of life there, so it has to be good. The food markets are alive with the freshest of produce, full of the season's splendour and ready to be lovingly prepared and cooked for the family. Seasonality is important to the Italians, and each ingredient is used just as it ripens, carefully and caringly prepared for the stunningly simple dishes that characterise the best of Italian cooking.

Even the rich Italian soil excites me. When I am in Italy, I constantly scour the landscape, feasting my eyes on the fields of golden wheat and corn, the herring-bone terraces of vines and the orchards of olives and lemons. As you travel south you start to smell the fertility of the land and see the fields alive with the colours of tomatoes, sweet peppers and aubergines.

Everything in Italy stops for the midday meal, which in itself signifies the importance of eating to the Italians. The streets are silent and, if you listen closely, the sound of knives and forks can be heard. There will also be laughing and arguing, for eating is a passionate affair. Any meal represents the essence of the Italian way of life – of living life to the full.

My book is about this splendid land and its splendid people. The simplicity of my dishes reflects the land, the seasons and the people. I'm passionate about flavour and tradition, and these are combined here, following extensive research the length and breadth of the country. Many of the recipes are traditional and long forgotten, while some are from my own family. They are all easy to prepare, and by cooking them and sharing them with family and friends you will be bringing the heart of Italy home to your own kitchen.

URSULA FERRIGNO

PRIMAVERA

spring

'And frosts are slain and flowers begotten,
And in green underwood and cover
Blossom by blossom the spring begins.'

Chorus from 'Atlanta in Calydon' Swinburne (1837–1909)

ASPARAGO

asparagus

Wild asparagus, asparago di campo or asparago selvatico, is indigenous to central and southern Europe, North Africa and western and central Asia. The plant belongs to the lily family. Frescoes in Egyptian royal tombs reveal that asparagus has been around for a long time, and the Ancient Romans also enjoyed it. Cato documents how to grow the plant, and there are a number of recipes in other classical sources. The name 'asparagus' is thought to come from the Persian, and it was the Arabs who introduced the vegetable to many parts of Europe.

The thick asparagus spears with which we are familiar are a cultivated form of the wild original. The spears or shoots of the wild plant are thin and spindly, thinner than the sprue you can find in British markets. These shoots form from a rootstock and, if left, will develop into a lacy mass of thin branches, up to 1.5m (5ft) high. There are male and female flowers, and the fruit is a red shiny berry that makes the plant look happy! Pigeons are said to be very fond of these berries, which is probably a major way
in which the plant spreads in the wild.

In cultivation, the thin shoots have been encouraged to become thicker. The French and Italians like their asparagus plump and white, so the shoots are blanched by heaping earth around them to keep them out of the sun. The British prefer green asparagus, so the shoots are exposed to the sun before cutting. There is never-ending debate as to which is best in flavour!

Asparagus, both wild and cultivated, is much loved in Italy. It is served simply: cold with oil and lemon juice, hot with melted butter and grated Parmesan. It is also used in omelettes, risottos and flans.

FRITTATA DI ASPARAGI
a s p a r a g u s   o m e l e t t e

Frittata is one of the easiest and tastiest recipes, using only the simplest of ingredients. I often cook it when I've just come back from holiday and there's nothing else in the fridge (apart from the chosen vegetable, of course). It's good eaten hot or at room temperature.

SERVES 2

250g (9oz) asparagus, trimmed and well washed

4 large eggs

1 garlic clove, peeled and crushed

a pinch of dried chilli (peperoncino)

2 tbsp whole milk

1 tbsp freshly grated Parmesan cheese

sea salt and freshly ground black pepper

2 tbsp olive oil

1 Preheat the oven to 200°C / 400°F / gas mark 6. Roast the asparagus for six minutes, turning once, then cut each spear in three.

2 Beat the eggs lightly and mix in the asparagus and all the remaining ingredients, apart from the oil.

3 Heat the olive oil in a medium-sized frying pan and, when hot, pour in the mixture. Let it set, shaking from time to time. Slide it out on to a flat lid or plate and quickly invert it into the hot pan to brown the other side. Alternatively cook the top side under the grill.

TORTA DI ASPARAGI
asparagus flan

Wrapped up in a clean napkin or in paper, this flan is easy to transport in a basket or hamper for a spring (or summer) picnic. It looks good, tastes good, and is wonderful with fruit, salad and wine. It's a real boon for the cook as it can be made ahead of time. (And the pastry is really simple to make – a real confidence booster!)

SERVES 6

Pastry:

150g (5½oz) Italian 00 plain flour

55g (2oz) unsalted butter

1 large egg, lightly beaten

3 tbsp whole milk

Filling:

375g (13oz) asparagus, trimmed and well washed

25g (1oz) unsalted butter

2 tbsp Italian 00 flour

4 large eggs, lightly beaten

250g (9oz) ricotta cheese, fresh if possible

2 garlic cloves, peeled and crushed

¼ tsp freshly grated nutmeg

55g (2oz) Parmesan cheese, freshly grated

sea salt and freshly ground black pepper

1 To make the pastry: combine the ingredients in a food processor. Gently knead on a work surface then wrap in greaseproof paper or cling film and chill for 30 minutes.

2 Heat the oven to 200°C / 400°F / gas mark 6.

3 To make the filling: bring a pot of water to a rapid boil. Add salt. Lower asparagus into the water and cook until just tender, three to six minutes. Transfer asparagus to a bowl of cold water.

4 Make a roux by melting the butter in a small heavy saucepan over a medium heat. Add the flour and stir until dissolved and foaming. Remove from the heat and let the roux cool.

5 Cut off the asparagus tips; set to one side. Cut the stems into 2cm (¾in) pieces; combine in a bowl with the eggs, ricotta, Parmesan, garlic, roux, nutmeg, salt and pepper.

6 On a lightly floured board, roll out two-thirds of the pastry into a 28cm (11in) round, 3mm (⅛in) thick. Line a 23cm (9in) tart tin with the pastry. Trim off excess dough and prick the bottom of the tart with a fork. Spread the filling evenly over the pastry and top with the asparagus tips. Roll out the remaining pastry into a smaller round also 3mm (⅛in) thick. Cut the pastry into 2cm (¾in) wide strips, using a fluted pastry wheel. Arrange the strips over the filling in a lattice pattern. Bake the flan in the preheated oven for 30 minutes until golden. Cool on a wire rack.

RISOTTO CON ASPARAGI SELVATICI

risotto with asparagus

Rice is a humble, basic food, but can be made into something really exotic like an Italian risotto, with a few twists such as adding wine, cheese and a seasonal vegetable. You could use any vegetable within reason, but the flavour of asparagus blends particularly well with rice. If wild asparagus is not available, use sprue or tender young spears, rather than the fat white ones, which can be a bit woody.

SERVES 6

500g (18oz) asparagus, trimmed and well washed

1 tbsp olive oil

150g (5½oz) unsalted butter

6 shallots, peeled and chopped

350g (12oz) vialone nano risotto rice

1 litre (1¾ pints) vegetable broth (see page 128), hot

7 tbsp white wine

100g (3½oz) Parmesan, freshly grated

a handful of fresh basil leaves

sea salt and freshly ground black pepper

1 Cut the tips off the asparagus and keep to one side. Cut the spears into three pieces.

2 Heat the oil and butter together in a deep-sided sauté pan. Sauté the shallots over a low heat for five minutes, stirring frequently. Add the chopped asparagus and cook over a low heat for about four minutes, then add the rice. Mix so that all the grains are glistening.

3 Add 3 tbsp of hot broth and stir until absorbed. Add the wine and continue stirring until you need more liquid. Add the hot broth a ladleful at a time, stirring well between each addition, and not adding more until the last ladle has been absorbed.

4 Continue cooking over a low heat for 18 minutes until all the stock has been absorbed the rice is al dente, with a little chalky centre in each grain. Add the asparagus tips about five minutes before the end of cooking.

5 Stir in the cheese, salt, pepper and basil, place the lid on the pan and leave to rest for four minutes. Then serve immediately.

CARCIOFI
globe artichokes

This giant thistle is related to the cardoon, and the part that we eat is the immature flower bud. There are two main varieties: those with a pointed head and prickly leaves, Spinosa sarda, and those with a rounded head and no prickles, Spinosa romanesco. In Italy during the short artichoke season, they are truly celebrated in the markets. The vendors will prepare them for you, dipping them into lemon for you to buy, rush home, cook quickly and enjoy.

To trim an artichoke of all its tough, inedible parts, begin by soaking it for 20 minutes in a large bowl of water acidulated with the juice of half a lemon. To prevent discoloration, use the other half of the lemon to rub the artichoke as the inner flesh is exposed. Begin at the base and snap off the dark green leaves. As the leaves become lighter in colour, remove only the green portion, leaving the tender yellow part closest to the base. Stop when the leaves are completely yellow. Cut off and discard 2.5cm (1in) from the top of the artichoke. Open it carefully to remove the prickly inner leaves and scrape out the fuzzy choke with a teaspoon. Rinse the artichoke under cold water then dip it into the acidulated water again. Most of the stem is edible. Trim off the dry end and remove the outer green casing, leaving only the tender white core. Trim away any additional dark green that remains on the artichoke and return it to the lemon water.

CARCIOFI RIPIENI
stuffed artichokes

I first tasted this recipe in Milan. If the cheeses specified here aren't available, please experiment. So long as the cheeses are strong, the recipe will work. The artichokes look amazing when they come to the table, and although the recipe might sound complicated, I assure you it's not!

SERVES 6

4 large globe artichokes

1 lemon, halved

3 tbsp olive oil

1 garlic clove, peeled and crushed

a handful of fresh flat-leaf parsley leaves, finely chopped

165ml (5½fl oz) vegetable broth (see page 128)

Stuffing:

55g (2oz) Parmesan cheese, freshly grated

40g (1½oz) Fontina cheese, shredded

25g (1oz) Taleggio cheese, finely diced

¼ tsp finely chopped garlic

a handful of fresh basil leaves, torn

2 tbsp olive oil

1 Preheat the oven to 180°C / 350°F / gas mark 4.

2 To make the stuffing: combine the three cheeses, garlic, basil and olive oil in a small bowl. Set aside.

3 Trim the artichokes, using the lemon as described on page 20. Remove the stems from the trimmed artichokes, coarsely chop them and set aside. Spoon the stuffing into the cavity of each artichoke, dividing the mixture evenly.

4 Heat the olive oil in a medium-sized casserole over a low heat and add the garlic. Add the parsley, broth and chopped artichoke stems, and simmer for 15 minutes. Arrange the stuffed artichokes in the casserole and cover the dish. Bake for 50 minutes or until the artichokes are tender. When tender, a small paring knife should slip in and out easily when inserted into the thickest part of the artichoke bottom. Serve immediately.

TORTA PASQUALINA
easter pie (from liguria)

Traditionally this Easter pie from Liguria has thirty-two layers of pastry to celebrate the years of Christ's life. However, I've simplified matters, and used fewer layers. It's still very impressive, extremely tasty, and can be eaten hot or cold.

SERVES 6

Pastry:

315g (10½oz) Italian 00 plain flour

extra virgin olive oil

1 large egg yolk mixed with 1 tbsp water, to glaze

Filling:

3 baby globe artichokes

500g (1lb 2oz) fresh spinach

4 tbsp olive oil

2 garlic cloves, peeled and crushed

7 large eggs

100g (3½oz) Parmesan cheese, freshly grated

200g (7oz) ricotta cheese

a handful of fresh marjoram leaves, chopped

a handful of fresh borage leaves, chopped

sea salt and freshly ground black pepper

1 Preheat the oven to 180°C / 350°F / gas mark 4.

2 To prepare the filling: cook the artichokes and spinach separately in boiling salted water until just tender. Drain the spinach thoroughly and coarsely chop. Slice the artichokes. Sauté them briefly together in the olive oil in a frying pan with the garlic. Mix in one beaten egg, the Parmesan, ricotta, herbs and salt and pepper to taste.

3 For the pastry: heap the flour on a board and make a well in the centre. Add 2 tbsp of the extra virgin olive oil and sufficient water – about 2–3 tbsp – to make a smooth, soft dough. Divide the dough into 18 pieces and roll out each piece into a very thin round large enough to cover the bottom of a 23cm (9in) pie dish. Stack nine of these sheets in the pie dish, brushing each with oil as you go.

4 Top with the vegetable and ricotta mixture and make six hollows in it. Break an egg into each of these hollows and cover with the rest of the pastry sheets, brushing each with oil as before.

5 Brush the top of the pie with the egg yolk glaze. Bake in the preheated oven for an hour until golden brown. Serve hot or cold.

CAROTE

carrots play a modest role as aromatic
rather than vegetable in Italian cooking, but
can be found whole in bollito misto and are
dipped raw into pinzimonio or bagna cauda.
Italian carrots are normally of modest size, but
in one village, Corsano, in the Salento, they are
grown to remarkable dimensions – survival of a
priapic rite. (There they are called 'la pastinaca'
rather than 'carota' and are rather pale in
colour.) On the feast of Santi Pati the engaged
youths seek out the largest carrots and offer
them with ceremony to their future brides.
Afterwards the size and splendour of the
prodigies are examined by the entire village,
amidst laughter and rude gestures, to decide
which youth has produced the winner.

CAROTE ARROSTO CON SALVIA
carrots roasted with sage

Sage is often thought of as a meat herb only, especially to accompany pork and liver in Italy,
but it also goes extraordinarily well with vegetables, particularly carrots. Sage grows in such
abundance (well, it does in Italy) that it's satisfying to find another delicious use for it.

SERVES 6

**900g (2lb) carrots, scraped and sliced
1cm (½in) thick**

6 garlic cloves, peeled

3 tbsp olive oil

**a medium handful of fresh sage leaves
(young ones are less pungent)**

sea salt and freshly ground black pepper

1 Preheat the oven to 200°C /400°F /gas
mark 6. Oil a rimmed baking tin that holds
the carrots and the garlic in a single layer.

2 Toss the carrots and whole garlic cloves
in a large bowl with the olive oil and sage.
Season with salt and pepper.

3 Transfer to the baking tin. Roast without
tossing for 30 minutes or until just tender.
Transfer to a serving dish and eat immediately.

GARGANELLI CON VERDURE DI STAGIONE

pasta with spring vegetables

I've chosen this particular pasta shape because its ridges help the pasta absorb the delicate spring flavours of the vegetables. The cream makes the sauce more subtle, which makes this dish very popular with children, especially my nieces and nephews!

SERVES 6

4 tbsp olive oil

2 medium carrots, scraped and diced

1 celery stick, scraped and diced

1 garlic clove, peeled and crushed

1 small red onion, peeled and chopped

2 small courgettes, diced

100g (3½oz) freshly shelled peas

2 ripe tomatoes, diced

1 tsp fresh thyme leaves

a handful of fresh basil leaves, torn

a handful of freshly chopped flat leaf parsley

sea salt and freshly ground black pepper

375g (13oz) garganelli (ridged pointed tubes), or penne rigate

2 tbsp double cream

freshly grated Parmesan cheese for serving

1 Heat the oil in a deep sauté pan and sauté the carrot, celery, garlic, onion, courgette and peas over a low heat for 10 minutes, stirring frequently, or until tender.

2 Add the tomato and cover. Cook over a low heat for about six minutes, then add the herbs and salt and pepper to taste.

3 Cook the garganelli in rolling boiling salted water for seven to 10 minutes according to packet instructions.

4 Toss the pasta in the vegetable sauce, adding the cream and cheese to taste. Serve immediately.

RIGATONI CON BROCCOLI
pasta with broccoli

Broccoli, cooked properly, is wonderful with pasta, especially when its distinctive flavour is enhanced by that of anchovies. There are many different varieties of anchovy available, but in my experience of teaching and cooking, marinated are the best. You can find them in tins at delicatessens: they come in olive oil and vinegar (slightly agrodolce, or sweet and sour), and their subtlety doesn't interfere too much with any other ingredient. They simply enrich flavours.

SERVES 6

200g (7oz) broccoli florets

1 red onion, peeled and finely chopped

2 tbsp olive oil

1 garlic clove, peeled and crushed

½ tsp dried chilli (peperoncino)

freshly grated zest of 2 unwaxed lemons

8 marinated anchovies, chopped

sea salt and freshly ground black pepper

300g (10½oz) rigatoni (short, ribbed pasta tubes)

100g (3½oz) dried breadcrumbs, toasted

a handful of fresh flat-leaf parsley leaves, roughly chopped

1 Steam the broccoli for eight minutes until just tender. Drain.

2 Sauté the onion in the oil until softened, then add the garlic, peperoncino, lemon zest and anchovies, and mix well. Season with salt and pepper.

3 Cook the pasta in plenty of boiling salted water, until al dente. Drain well.

4 Mix the broccoli and onion mixture with the pasta, add the breadcrumbs and parsley, and serve immediately.

BROCCOLI

broccoli is a brassica, of the same family as cabbage, cauliflower and Brussels sprouts. It is thought to be the result of cultivation, of trying to grow cabbage with shoots, and the name 'broccoli' actually means 'little arms' or 'little shoots' in Italian. There are two principal types of broccoli: calabrese (originally from Calabria) has large, densely packed blue and green 'flowers' and few outer leaves, and sprouting broccoli is leafier with smaller, looser purple or white heads. The season for sprouting broccoli is February to May, and for calabrese from June to November. Broccoli is an excellent source of vitamin C, more so even than oranges, and it is also rich in vitamins A and B. However, it must be properly cooked to retain these properties. Steaming for just a few minutes over boiling salted water is best. When choosing broccoli, make sure it looks firm and healthy with stalks that are neither unduly woody nor dry and wrinkled. The heads should be tightly packed with no sign of yellowing. To prepare it for cooking peel the stalk only if it is thick and tough.

LATTUGA

lettuces now come in a whole range of colours, from the palest green iceberg to the rich russet brown of lollo rosso or oakleaf. Whatever type you buy, the same signs of freshness and quality apply: the leaves should be firm and crisp with no browning at the edges and no sign of slime or insect damage. When preparing them discard any wilted outer leaves, carefully wash the leaves you are using and dry them thoroughly by draining them on a clean tea-towel or in a salad spinner. Use most lettuces within a couple of days: this is especially relevant if they are straight from the garden as they are more fragile, having been grown with fewer insecticides and pesticides.

INSALATA DI RUCOLA CON FAVE
rocket salad with broad beans

Try to seek out different varieties of rocket to find which you like best. I'm not too keen on the rocket leaves you find in plastic bags, and would much rather go to my local market and buy bunches tied up with rubber bands as they do in Italy. The very thin leaves tend to be the wild ones; fatter leaves are what my father calls 'domestica' or cultivated. The wild in my mind is superior because of its fierce peppery flavour, and it goes very well with young – they must be young – broad beans.

SERVES 6

300g (10½oz) rocket, selvatica wild variety

300g (10½oz) oakleaf lettuce

125g (4½oz) young Pecorino Toscano, thinly sliced

675g (1½lb) young shelled broad beans

sea salt and freshly ground black pepper

4 tbsp fruity extra virgin olive oil

1 Combine the rocket and lettuce in a large shallow bowl.

2 Place the cheese on top, then scatter with the beans. Add some salt and pepper and the oil, and toss. Serve immediately.

SCAROLA CON PISTACCHI
escarole with pistachio nuts (from sicily)

Escarole is a slightly bitter lettuce which in southern Italy – particularly Sicily, where this recipe originates – is often served as a cooked vegetable. If you haven't eaten it this way before, you'll be delighted at the results. Adding the pistachios not only contributes colour but great texture as well.

SERVES 6

1kg (2¼lb) escarole or curly endive

50ml (2fl oz) olive oil

3 garlic cloves, peeled and chopped

sea salt and freshly ground black pepper

100g (3½oz) shelled pistachio nuts

1 Trim the escarole, discarding tough stems and damaged or wilted leaves. Cut each bunch into quarters, wash well and dry.

2 Heat the oil in a frying pan, add the garlic and cook lightly over a medium heat.

3 Add the escarole, cover and reduce the heat and cook for five minutes. Season with salt and pepper.

4 Scatter the pistachios on top and toss for another two minutes before serving.

PATATE

potatoes

Like the tomato and the pepper, which belong to the same botanical family, the potato was one of the edible treasures introduced to Europe from South America by the Spanish invaders. But it took 200 years for it to be really accepted, and only gradually did potatoes become an important food source throughout Europe. The potato can be grown at a higher altitude and in colder climates than any other food crop except barley, and is said to produce more food per acre than any other northern food crop. It came originally from the Andes, where the Incas were familiar with it 2,000 years ago. Today it is still an important crop in Peru, Ecuador and Colombia.

The potato is a tuber, which forms on rhizomes (underground stems), several to a single plant. Potatoes are sold in their skins, sometimes loose, sometimes packaged, sometimes washed, sometimes not. In shape and size they vary enormously, according to variety. The colour of the skin ranges from an almost parchment-like cream through yellow, brown, pink and red. The skin texture can be smooth or netted. The flesh colour varies from milky white to cream, pale yellow, deep yellow or pinkish yellow – and there are some 'black' potatoes! According to variety and crop, the texture of the flesh can be waxy or floury, and both are used in Italian cooking.

There can be few more versatile vegetables than the potato. It can be cooked almost any way you can imagine. The flavour and texture are restrained, which makes the potato a perfect vehicle and accompaniment for many other foods. The potato is nutritious, being an important source of vitamin C, complex carbohydrates and dietary fibre. It is also low in calories (it's the butter you melt on it that is fattening!).

When buying potatoes, look for the freshest, and newly dug potatoes are truly wonderful. If they are 'new', the skin should rub away easily and will probably already be flaking off. The skin will look tight as if the potatoes are bursting with freshness. Main-crop potatoes should be damage free, clean with smooth tight skins. Do not buy if the skins feel dry and wrinkled when you touch them. Neither should you buy any that are beginning to sprout or that are turning green. This means they have been exposed to light and toxins are being formed under the skin. Store all potatoes in a cool, dark, airy place in a brown paper bag, not plastic.

PATATE RIFATTE

potatoes 'done again'

When we say 'rifatte', it usually means 'cooked twice'. But for this recipe the verb 'cooked' is misused because the potatoes we use are raw. This is a culinary tradition dating back to times long ago when poor people expanded leftovers by adding further ingredients, in this case raw potatoes.

SERVES 4

3 tbsp olive oil

1 large red onion, peeled and finely chopped

2 garlic cloves, peeled and crushed

5 fresh sage leaves

5 large potatoes (such as the Spunta variety) peeled and cut into small chunks

a handful of fresh basil leaves

sea salt and freshly ground black pepper

1 x 225g (8oz) can plum tomatoes, drained and chopped

a handful of fresh flat-leaf parsley leaves, chopped

1 Heat the oil in a large sauté pan. Add the onion and cook until golden. Add the garlic, sage and potatoes and cook for five minutes more. Add 2 tbsp of water if too dry.

2 Stir in the tomatoes, basil, salt, and pepper. Cook on a medium heat, covered, for 15 minutes or until the potatoes are tender.

3 Serve sprinkled with parsley.

PATATE IN INSALATA DI SICILIA
sicilian potato salad

This salad is a real feast for the eyes and palate. It's full of crunch and flavour, and keeps very well (useful for our busy lives). I first enjoyed it on a trip with family friends to Syracuse, a beautiful fishing village. All these flavours are very characteristic of Sicilian cooking.

SERVES 4

6 Italian new potatoes (Spunta, Elvira or Nicola) scrubbed

a handful of salted capers, rinsed

8 pomodorini cherry tomatoes on the vine (when they are sweeter)

4 marinated anchovies, roughly chopped

8 marinated black olives

1 small red onion, peeled and roughly sliced

sea salt and freshly ground black pepper

3 tbsp fruity extra virgin olive oil

a sprinkling of fresh oregano leaves

1 Peel the potatoes, cut into 2.5cm (1in) chunks and boil for about about six to eight minutes until tender. Drain and leave to cool.

2 Add the capers to the cooled potatoes, plus the tomatoes, anchovies, olives and onion.

3 Season with salt and pepper, add the oil and oregano and mix well. Serve at room temperature.

GNOCCHI DI PATATE

potato gnocchi

The word 'gnocco', literally translated, means 'little lump', which is precisely what a gnocco is. There are so many poor imitations ready-prepared for us to buy, that I urge you to spend some time making them yourself. The results are infinitely superior, and it's certainly not difficult (in fact, it's fun!). We use old potatoes here, rather than the waxy new, because the starch is fully developed, and therefore allows the gnocchi to cohere, to stay together. The gnocchi are also lighter in texture. The classical way to enjoy potato gnocchi is with a home-made tomato sauce, but they're also good with a walnut sauce (see page 168).

SERVES 4

Gnocchi:

225–275g (8–10oz) Italian 00 plain flour

2 small eggs

900g (2lb) even-sized old potatoes (Maris Piper, King Edward, Desirée)

sea salt

55g (2oz) unsalted softened butter, cubed

freshly grated Parmesan to serve

Tomato sauce:
(makes about 300ml (½ pint))

1 tbsp olive oil

1 small onion, peeled and finely chopped

450g (1lb) ripe tomatoes or a 400g (14oz) can Italian plum tomatoes

1 garlic clove, peeled and crushed

150ml (¼ pint) vegetable broth (see page 128) or water

1 tbsp tomato purée

a pinch of caster sugar

a handful of fresh basil leaves (optional), torn

sea salt and freshly ground black pepper

1 tbsp dry white wine

1 Make the sauce first. If using fresh tomatoes, put them in a bowl, cover with boiling water for 30 seconds then plunge into cold water. Using a sharp knife, peel off the skins, cut in half, discard the seeds, then roughly chop the flesh.

2 Heat the oil in a saucepan, add the onion and cook gently for five minutes until softened. Add the tomatoes and garlic, cover and cook over a gentle heat for 10 minutes, stirring occasionally.

3 Add the stock or water, tomato purée, sugar, basil (if using) and salt and pepper to taste. Half cover the pan and simmer for 20 minutes, stirring occasionally.

4 Sieve the tomato mixture into a clean pan. Bring to the boil, add the wine and keep to one side, off the heat.

5 For the gnocchi: meanwhile, cook the potatoes in their skins in boiling water for 20 minutes until tender (or longer, depending on size). Drain well and when cool enough to handle, peel off the skins.

6 Seive the flour into a bowl and make a well in the centre. Crack the eggs into the well.

7 Push the potatoes through a seive on to the flour and eggs, from a height to enable the potato to lighten with air as it falls. Add plenty of salt and the butter. Mix thoroughly and then knead until soft, adding more flour if necessary.

8 With floured hands, roll the dough into 2.5cm (1in) thick rolls, then cut into pieces about 2cm (¾in) long. Press a finger into each piece to flatten then draw your finger towards you to curl the sides.

9 Bring a large pan of salted water to the boil and drop in about 20 gnocchi. Lower the heat and cook gently for two to three minutes, allowing the gnocchi to pop to the top of the pan and counting for 30 seconds. Remove the gnocchi with a slotted spoon and keep warm. Repeat with the remaining gnocchi.

10 Warm up the tomato sauce. When all the gnocchi are cooked, toss in the sauce and serve sprinkled with Parmesan cheese.

SCHIACCIATA DOLCE
sweet flatbread

I published this recipe in Truly Italian, and have since used it in my workshops, where it has been very successful and popular. As a result, I couldn't resist repeating it again here. Schiacciata means 'squashed' or 'flattened', and there are many variations on the theme throughout Italy. This bread, made with a batter-like dough, has a slightly sweet flavour, and is perfect warm for breakfast, or for tea.

MAKES 1 LARGE LOAF

175ml (6fl oz) water (hand hot), plus 2 tbsp

15g (½oz) fresh yeast

280g (10oz) strong white unbleached flour, plus extra for dusting

1 tsp olive oil

1 large egg, lightly beaten

150g (5½oz) unsalted butter, melted

40g (1½oz) caster sugar

1 tbsp each of finely grated unwaxed orange and lemon zests

¼ tsp saffron powder

1 tbsp vanilla extract

vanilla icing sugar for dusting

ZAFFERANO

saffron consists of dried crocus stigmas and some 70,000 flowers need to be hand-picked to get 450g (1lb). It has a spicy, bitter taste, and a pungent odour, so only small quantities are needed. In Italy it is the classic flavouring of Risotto Milanese.

1 Pour all the water into a bowl. Add the yeast and stir to dissolve, then leave for 5 minutes to froth. Gradually add the measured flour and mix with your hands until a ball of dough is formed. Knead the dough vigorously on a lightly floured surface.

2 Oil a bowl. Turn the dough in the oil to coat it. Cover the bowl and leave the dough to rise until doubled in size, about an hour.

3 Punch the dough down in the bowl, then add the egg and all but 2 tbsp of the melted butter, the sugar, zests, saffron and vanilla. Use a wooden spoon to gently mix the ingredients. Mix for 10 minutes, adding more flour if necessary.

5 Use half the remaining melted butter to grease a baking sheet with a lip, measuring 30 x 25cm (12 x 10in). Using a spatula, pour the dough on to the prepared sheet, and smooth it out to the edges. Brush the remaining melted butter over the top. Let the dough rise in a warm place, covered, for about 1½ hours.

6 Preheat the oven to 200°C / 400°F / gas mark 6. Bake the bread for 20–25 minutes until nicely golden on top. Cool on a wire rack. Cut into squares and dust with icing sugar.

RISOTTO AL SALTO
crisp risotto cake

When Milanese cooks have some risotto left over, they sauté it in a very thin layer until it is golden and crisp. You could serve by itself as here, or as a crunchy lid for a piping hot, creamy risotto. It's appropriate here because the colour of the risotto is yellow, signifying spring!

SERVES 6

1 Melt 85g (3oz) of the butter in a sauté pan, add the shallot and sauté until golden. Add the rice and cook for a few moments to let it absorb the fat and shallot flavour.

2 Add the wine and cook until evaporated. Dissolve the saffron in a tbsp of the hot vegetable broth and add to the rice.

3 Season with pepper; cook for 15 minutes, adding the remaining broth a little at a time, stirring constantly with a wooden spoon. At the end of this time, the rice should be fairly dry. Season with salt. Spread the rice on a board and let it stand until cooled.

4 Melt half the remaining butter in a frying pan. Cover the bottom with a layer of rice 6mm (¼in) thick, pressing down lightly. Brown over a low heat for 20 minutes.

5 Invert the rice cake on to a flat saucepan lid or a plate for a moment. Add the remaining butter to the frying pan. Slide the rice back into the pan and brown the other side, shaking the pan to prevent sticking.

6 Place the rice cake on a serving plate and sprinkle with Parmesan. Serve at once as an antipasto, cut into wedges.

140g (5oz) unsalted butter

3 shallots, peeled and finely chopped

300g (10½oz) vialone nano rice

120ml (4fl oz) dry white wine

¼ tsp saffron

1 litre (1¾ pints) vegetable broth (see page 128)

sea salt & freshly ground black pepper

6 tbsp freshly grated Parmesan cheese

MENTA

mint grows all over the world, in the wild as well as in cultivation. There are many varieties, which are difficult to differentiate since they hybridise very easily. Some of the most common are spearmint (Mentha spicata, and the mint for cooks), peppermint (M. piperita, a hybrid between M. aquatica or watermint and spearmint), pennyroyal (M. pulegium) and apple mint (M. rotundifolia). Mint is perhaps my favourite herb, and I use it extensively in my cooking. For me its unique flavour blends so well with southern Italian ingredients, doing wonders for courgettes, tomatoes, potatoes, sauces, marinades and fish. It also makes a great mint pesto for pasta, gnocchi and risotto.

FRITTATA DI ERBE SELVATICHE
wild herb omelette

I love frittata, as it is such a spontaneous food – most kitchens will have the basic ingredients. This recipe is best if you have access to lots of herbs from the garden, and you can randomly select your own favourites.

SERVES 4

4 large eggs

1 garlic clove, peeled and crushed

1 tsp fresh thyme leaves, chopped

a handful of fresh basil leaves, torn

a handful of fresh mint leaves, chopped

1 tsp chopped fresh rosemary leaves

sea salt and freshly ground black pepper

3 tbsp olive oil

1 medium white onion, peeled and finely chopped

1 Whisk thoroughly the eggs, garlic, herbs, salt and pepper in a large bowl.

2 Heat the oil in a large frying pan about 25cm (10in) in diameter over a medium heat. Add the chopped onion and cook until lightly golden. Add the egg mixture and cook over a medium heat until the bottom is golden.

3 Heat the grill and cook the top of the frittata gently for about six minutes until golden and puffy. Serve immediately, cut into wedges.

GNOCCHI DI PANE
bread gnocchi

In Italy a good cook never wastes anything. As bread stales so quickly, many recipes have been created to utilise it. These bread gnocchi are very light and full of herby flavour, and are delicious with a tomato or pesto sauce.

SERVES 6

250g (9oz) stale bread, crusts discarded, finely chopped

a handful of fresh mint leaves, torn

1 tsp each of finely chopped fresh marjoram, thyme and rosemary leaves

1 tsp minced rosemary

140g (5oz) Parmesan cheese, freshly grated

2 large eggs, beaten

2-3 tbsp whole milk

a generous pinch of freshly grated nutmeg

sea salt and freshly ground black pepper

Italian 00 plain flour for dusting

To serve:

250g (9oz) tomato sauce with mint (see page 43)

a handful of rocket leaves, cut into strips

shavings of Parmesan (optional)

1 To make the gnocchi, combine the bread, herbs, cheese, eggs, milk, nutmeg, salt and pepper. Knead until the mixture holds together. Add somemore milk if the mixture is too dry or some of the flour if it is too wet.

2 Turn the mixture out on to a floured work surface and cut into 4 pieces. Shape each piece into 2.5cm (1in) thick logs, and cut each log into 1cm (½in) pieces.

3 Cook the gnocchi in a large pan of boiling, salted water until they float to the surface. Count 30 seconds then remove with a slotted spoon to a heated bowl.

4 Fold in the warmed tomato sauce and top with the rocket. You may like to serve them with extra shavings of Parmesan. I often add a fine drizzle of exceptional extra virgin olive oil.

SALSA DI POMODORI CON MENTA
tomato sauce with mint

I have a passion for mint and tomatoes, as they are such great partners. I first enjoyed this combination in Sicily, one breathtakingly hot lunchtime.

SERVES 6

500g (1lb 2oz) fresh sun-ripened tomatoes

1 onion, peeled and chopped

2-3 fresh bay leaves

1 dsp capers, rinsed

2 handfuls fresh mint leaves

2 garlic cloves, peeled

1 tsp caster sugar

sea salt and freshly ground black pepper

1 tsp dried chilli (peperoncino)

2 tbsp extra virgin olive oil (estate bottled and fruity)

1 Cut the tomatoes into quarters. Heat the oil in a medium-sized saucepan and cook the tomatoes with the onion and bay leaves for 20 minutes. Remove the bay and press the tomatoes through a sieve or foodmill (mouli di legume). Return the sauce to the pan and simmer for 25 minutes to thicken.

2 While the sauce is cooking, blend the capers, mint and garlic together and set aside.

3 When the sauce is almost ready, add the sugar, salt and pepper and chilli. Taste and adjust the seasoning. Cook on a very low heat for 10 minutes. Turn off the heat and stir in the mint mixture and the oil. The sauce is now ready.

GRANCEOLA AL LIMONE
crab with lemon

Granceole are large, very tender spider crabs found only in Venice, where they are considered a delicacy. They are served simply with lemon so as not to overwhelm their subtle flavour. Please feel free to use other crabs though.

SERVES 6

6 spider crabs, about 200g (7oz) each

18 lettuce leaves

125ml (4fl oz) extra virgin olive oil

juice of 1-2 lemons

a handful of fresh flat-leaf parsley leaves, finely chopped

sea salt and freshly ground black pepper

1 Bring a saucepan of salted water to the boil and drop in the crabs (still alive if possible). Cook for 10 minutes, or until pink in colour, then leave to cool in the cooking water.

2 Make a circular cut beneath the upper shells of the main body and take out the flesh. Remove and discard the entrails and stomach, reserving the coral if there is any. Clean out the inside of each shell and wash well.

3 Place three lettuce leaves on each plate and top with the crab shells. Mix the crabmeat with the oil, lemon juice, parsley and a little salt and pepper. Return the flesh to the shells. Scatter the coral (if any) over each filled shell, and serve.

GRANCHIO

crab is much loved in Italy, and many of the best recipes come from around Venice. There the spider crab reigns supreme. This curious looking creature has five sets of legs with two minuscule claws that are arranged around the body like the legs of a spider. Its shell is covered in sharp bumps. Large crabs and other smaller crabs are also enjoyed, the latter in fish soups and stews. Crab flesh can be eaten 'dressed' as here, or in seafood salads or pasta sauces.

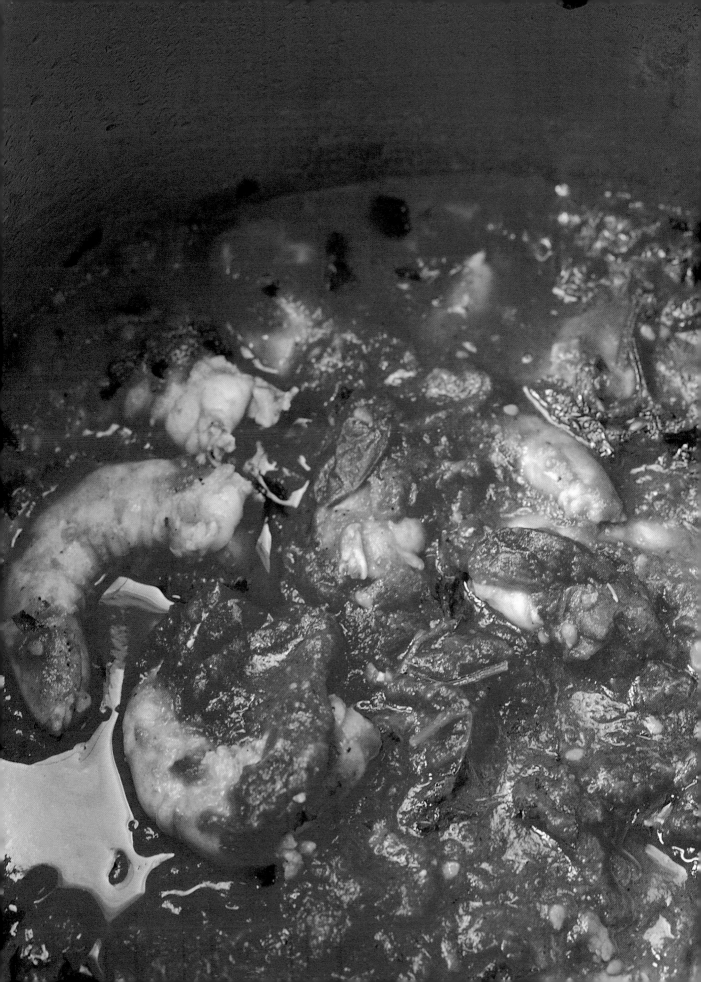

GAMBERI/GAMBERETTI

prawns *vary in size and colour, ranging from the translucent, almost transparent pink of the small common prawn, to the deep blue-brown of the raw giant or tiger prawn. They come from cold and warm waters; the large are generally warm-water, and are mostly seen frozen. Try to buy them raw and in the shell, as the shell ensures they retain some succulence (and the shells can be used in a fish broth). Whatever kind you choose, my best advice is fresh, fresh, fresh: you must always find a reliable supplier. Prawns can be stir-fried, steamed, or added to a sauce for pasta or risotto. They are also wonderful in a seafood salad.*

SPAGHETTI ALLA CASORZA
spaghetti with prawns

This is definitely one of the quickest, tastiest and simplest recipes and I first enjoyed it in a little seaside town in Liguria. It's so easy to replicate at home, but you must ensure that you use the very best-quality ingredients. I think this could easily become part of your weekly repertoire!

SERVES 6

400g (14oz) raw tiger or king prawns, the best and freshest you can find

4 tbsp olive oil

2 garlic cloves, peeled and crushed

a handful of fresh flat-leaf parsley leaves, roughly chopped

1 medium chilli, finely chopped

5 tbsp dry white wine

300g (10½oz) canned Italian plum tomatoes, chopped

350g (12oz) spaghetti

sea salt and freshly ground black pepper

1 Shell and clean the prawns.

2 Heat the oil in a large casserole and add the garlic, parsley and chilli, stirring constantly so as not to burn them. Now add the prawns and cook for one minute. Stir in the wine and tomatoes and cook for two to three minutes.

3 Meanwhile cook the pasta in plenty of rolling boiling salted water.

4 Drain the pasta, add to the pan with the sauce, season to taste and serve immediately.

TEGLIA DI SPADA
marinated swordfish

When truly fresh, this is awesomely good. Swordfish is mainly caught in the channel that separates Sicily and Africa. The fish is often cooked on the brace or barbecue/grill and served with lemon and capers.

SERVES 6

6 swordfish steaks, about 175g (6oz) each

sea salt and freshly ground black pepper

250ml (9fl oz) dry white wine

1 sprig fresh rosemary

4 garlic cloves, peeled and finely chopped

a handful of fresh mint leaves, chopped

4 tbsp olive oil

100g (3½oz) fine dried breadcrumbs

3 tbsp capers, salted, rinsed and chopped

juice of 1 lemon

1 Place the swordfish steaks in a bowl and season with salt and pepper. Pour over the wine. Finely chop the rosemary leaves and add to the fish with the garlic and mint. Coat the steaks, and marinate for at least an hour.

2 Drain the fish reserving the marinade. Brush a large frying pan with a little oil and heat it. Sprinkle the steaks with a mixture of the breadcrumbs and capers. Add the steaks, two or three at a time, to the frying pan and cook on both sides until nearly cooked through, basting with the marinade. This should take about eight minutes altogether.

3 Whisk the rest of the oil with the lemon juice in a small bowl. Pour over the fish and cook for a few minutes more. This keeps the fish tender. Serve immediately.

PESCE SPADA

swordfish used to be prolific in the Mediterranean, especially off the Calabrian coast and around Sicily, but they have been overfished, and supplies now usually come from other parts of the world. Swordfish are aggressive and solitary, and they can grow to great size. No-one seems to be quite sure of the purpose of the sword...

Steaks of pale peachy-pink swordfish meat are occasionally available. The best time to buy swordfish is in late spring, although it is available all year round. The fish, which cooks white, has a fine meaty texture, but is inclined to dryness and should be marinated before cooking, and it must never be overcooked. Steaks can be breaded and fried like veal, baked, or grilled on the barbecue (when it is wonderful with a chilled tangy salsa).

PESCI SERRA AI FIORI DI ZUCCA
fish wrapped in courgette flowers

This is a recipe for late spring, early summer, and it is bright in colour, very dramatic when presented at the table and full of simple good flavours. Courgette blossoms are available to buy at your greengrocer (order them in advance any time from May through June) or best, grow them yourself.

SERVES 6

1 Slice four of the courgettes lengthwise, 2mm (⅟₁₆in) thick, using a large chef's knife. You should have 24 slices.

2 Fill a large pan with water and bring it to the boil. Add salt. Blanch the courgettes in the boiling water for two minutes or until flexible.

3 Shred the remaining four courgettes. Heat the olive oil in a large sauté pan over a medium heat. Add the shredded courgette, garlic and wine and boil briskly for two minutes. Season with salt and pepper. Set to one side.

4 Cut the fish into 24 pieces about 6cm (2½in) long and 1cm (½in) wide. Season with salt and pepper.

5 Ease the courgette blossoms open and remove the stamens. Rinse them under cold water and pat dry with paper towels. Brush the inside of each with beaten egg and wrap it lengthwise around a piece of fish. Wrap a slice of blanched courgette around the centre of each piece and arrange the fish parcels on top of the shredded courgette in the pan.

6 Cover the pan and simmer for seven to 10 minutes or until the fish is cooked.

8 medium courgettes, trimmed

4 tbsp olive oil

2 medium garlic cloves, peeled and crushed

175ml (6fl oz) dry white wine

sea salt and freshly ground black pepper

675g (1½lb) swordfish steaks, 2.5cm (1in) thick, skin removed

24 courgette blossoms

1 large egg, beaten

LIMONE

lemon

The lemon is a member of the tropical and sub-tropical Citrus family. The fruit form on small trees of about 3–6m (10–20ft) high, and often stay green in the tropics, rather than turn the familiar yellow. The citrus group probably originated in China and south-east Asia, although the lemon is thought to have developed in India. It was gradually introduced westwards. When the Roman Empire extended into the East, lemons began to be grown in Rome, but general knowledge of the lemon did not spread to the rest of Italy until the fourth century, and did not reach France and Spain until the Middle Ages. At the end of the tenth century, the lemon began to be used for medicinal purposes in Muslim countries. Avicenna, the prince of physicians, prescribed it for the ailments suffered by pregnant women, indigestion and vomiting.

In modern times the fruit is not considered to possess such legendary virtues, yet it has undoubtedly earned a remarkable scientific reputation. Many medical experts have acknowledged the bacteriological action of its acidic components, which also prevent the process of oxidation – a cut apple or globe artichoke turning brown.

The positive effect of its high content of vitamin C has long been recognised. British sailors, who used to suffer from a vitamin C deficiency disease called scurvy, were 'cured' when the fruit's valuable properties were discovered in the late eighteenth century. (The lime was issued to seamen as well, resulting in the Americans nicknaming the British 'limeys'.)

But it is in cooking that lemons are most useful, their acidity lending flavour and enhancing flavour. In Italy lemon is a fundamental ingredient, used in almost everything – in sweets and savouries and also in the household. My grandfather used to say, 'Lemons, they are medicine'.

BROCCOLI AL LIMONE ED ERBE
broccoli dressed with lemon and herbs

For me this vegetable is magically characteristic of Italian food – plainly cooked, simply dressed, and delicious. Don't waste any of the dressing: mop it up Italian style with a scarpetta, 'little shoe', of bread.

SERVES 4

500g (1lb 2oz) broccoli, divided into large florets

sea salt and freshly ground black pepper

Dressing:

1 onion, peeled and finely chopped

6 garlic cloves, peeled and finely chopped

2 sprigs fresh thyme, leaves stripped from the stalks

2 tbsp finely chopped fresh flat-leaf parsley

finely grated zest and juice of 2 lemons

125ml (4fl oz) olive oil

1 First make the dressing for the broccoli. Put all the ingredients into a jar, shake vigorously and leave to macerate (the longer the better). Strain before use.

2 Steam the broccoli until al dente.

3 Dress the broccoli with the lemon and herb dressing whilst still warm. Serve immediately.

PASTIERA
easter pie

Pastiera is the traditional Neapolitan Easter pastry. Each family has its own recipe and discusses it at length with friends and neighbours, everybody tasting each other's and commenting on them all. This pastry is offered to guests for at least a week around Easter time. It is traditionally left in the pan in which it is baked, never turned out.

SERVES 8

Pastry:

250g (9oz) Italian 00 plain flour

125g (4½oz) unsalted butter, softened

55g (2oz) golden caster sugar

1 large egg yolk

Filling:

150g (5½oz) whole wheat kernels (from a health-food store)

325ml (11fl oz) whole milk

finely grated zest of 4 lemons (or 2 oranges)

115g (4oz) golden caster sugar

1 tsp vanilla extract

250g (9oz) ricotta cheese

3 large egg yolk

2 tbsp chopped candied citron peel

1 tbsp chopped candied orange peel

1 tbsp chopped candied pumpkin (optional)

a generous pinch of ground cinnamon

2 large egg whites

1 Soak the wheat in cold water overnight.

2 For the pastry, combine the flour, butter, sugar and egg yolk to make a dough. Form into a ball. Let rest while preparing the filling.

3 Drain the wheat and combine with the milk, lemon zest and 1 tbsp of the sugar and cook over a low heat until the mixture is creamy and porridge-like. Remove from the heat and stir in the vanilla. Leave to cool.

4 Preheat the oven to 180°C / 350°F / gas mark 4.

5 Combine the ricotta, three egg yolks, the remaining sugar, the wheat mixture, candied fruit and cinnamon. Beat the egg whites until stiff and fold into the mixture.

6 Roll out three-quarters of the pastry dough and use it to line a 23cm (9in) spring-form tin. Fill with the ricotta mixture. Roll out the remaining dough and cut it into 1cm (½in) strips with a fluted pastry wheel.

7 Arrange the strips in a lattice over the filling and crimp the edges. Bake the pastiera in the preheated oven for 1 hour or until the pastry is golden brown. Let cool before serving.

TORTA DI LIMONE I
lemon cake I

Potato flour is available from health-food stores, and gives a very light texture. It's well worth investigating because it really does enhance all cakes. In Italy vanilla icing sugar can be bought pre-prepared and comes in wonderful, old-fashioned waxed paper cones. However you can make it yourself simply by inserting a vanilla pod into a container of icing sugar and leaving it to infuse.

SERVES 6

12 large eggs, separated

200g (7oz) golden caster sugar

finely grated zest and juice of 4 unwaxed lemons

finely grated zest of 1 orange

150g (5½oz) freshly shelled walnuts, chopped

115g (4oz) potato flour

175g (6oz) Italian 00 plain flour

¼ tsp fine sea salt

vanilla icing sugar for dusting

1 Preheat the oven to 170°C / 325°F / gas mark 3. Grease a 25cm (10in) cake tin.

2 Using an electric mixer, beat the egg yolks until pale and foamy.

3 Beat in the sugar then add the lemon juice, orange and lemon zest and the walnuts. Mix until smooth.

4 Sift the flours and salt together and fold into the yolk mixture.

5 Beat the egg whites until stiff and fold into the yolk mixture.

6 Spoon into the prepared cake tin and bake in the preheated oven for an hour.

7 Turn out and cool on a wire rack and dust with vanilla icing sugar.

TORTA DI LIMONE II
lemon cake II

This recipe is for all cheesecake lovers. The flavour is very intense. Cottage cheese is the nearest I have found to create the texture I am looking for, because the cheese my aunt uses is only available in the south of Italy.

SERVES 6

Biscuit base:

250g (9oz) digestive biscuits (organic ones are best – less sweet, more honeyed)

finely grated zest of 1 unwaxed lemon

1 tsp ground cinnamon

115g (4oz) unsalted butter, melted

Filling:

125g (4½oz) cottage cheese, sieved

250g (9oz) full-fat cream cheese

100g (3½oz) caster sugar

3 large drops vanilla extract

2 large eggs, beaten

finely grated zest of 3 lemons

1 tsp lemon juice

100ml (3½fl oz) double cream

freshly grated nutmeg

1 Preheat the oven to 180°C / 350°F / gas mark 4.

2 For the base, put the biscuits into a plastic bag, and smash to crumbs with a rolling pin. Place in a bowl and mix in the lemon zest, cinnamon and melted butter.

3 Turn the biscuit mixture into a 20cm (8in) spring-form tin and press firmly and evenly over the base. Chill until needed.

4 Put the sieved cottage cheese into a large mixing bowl, beat in the cream cheese and then add the sugar and vanilla. Beat in the eggs so that the mixture is a pouring consistency. Add the lemon zest and mix well.

5 Pour the mixture on top of the biscuit base in the tin and bake in the preheated oven for 25 minutes.

6 Take the cake out of the oven and increase the oven heat to 230°C / 450°F / gas mark 8. Meanwhile, mix the lemon juice with the cream and pour on top of the baked mixture. Sprinkle the surface lightly with nutmeg and return to the very hot oven for five minutes.

7 Leave the cheesecake on the tray to cool and firm up for a good six to eight hours before serving.

CREMA DI LATTE

lemon cream

This blancmange-like custard looks wonderful served with fresh seasonal fruit, particularly with cherries and apricots which are available in Italy earlier than they are in England. Some new fresh figs would be wonderful later on in the year.

SERVES 6

1 Pass the egg yolks through a sieve into a large heavy saucepan. Add the sugar and blend with a wire balloon whisk. Add the flour and stir until it is completely absorbed.

2 Slowly pour in the milk and stir vigorously until the mixture is smooth. Place pan over a gentle heat, add the lemon rind and cook, stirring constantly, about 20 minutes, until the custard has thickened.

3 Pour the custard into a bowl. Remove the zest. Place a buttered round of waxed paper on the surface to prevent a skin forming. When cool, cover the bowl with clingfilm and refrigerate.

4 Remove the custard from the refrigerator 15 minutes before serving. Spoon it into a serving bowl and sprinkle with cinnamon. Serve with seasonal fruit.

5 large egg yolks

150g (5½oz) caster sugar

85g (3oz) Italian 00 plain flour

1 litre (1¾ pints) whole milk

rind of 1 unwaxed lemon, pared in one long strip

pinch of ground cinnamon

LIMONCELLO
lemon liqueur

This liqueur is made throughout the whole of southern Italy. As flavour is so important, always use unwaxed lemons. In Italy we use pure alcohol, which is difficult to obtain in the UK. A high proof vodka is a good alternative, as it has a neutral flavour. This liqueur is good after a meal if you like the sweetness, and some Italians love it poured over their gelato. My aunt makes it still, to her own specific recipe, and never reveals her secret ingredient. (We think it's mint leaves...)

SERVES 6

6 unwaxed lemons

a 75cl (25fl oz) bottle vodka (or pure alcohol)

225g (8oz) caster sugar

450ml (¾ pint) pure bottled water

1 Put the lemons in one bowl of cold water and leave to soak for one hour. Remove from the water and dry with kitchen paper.

2 Using a vegetable peeler, carefully peel the rind from the lemons, taking care not to remove the white pith.

3 Put the lemon rind in a wide-mouthed jar. Pour over the vodka and cover. Leave in a dark place for 20 days.

4 After 20 days, put the sugar and the bottled water in a saucepan and bring to the boil, stirring to dissolve the sugar. Remove from the heat, cover and leave until cold.

5 When cold, add the sugar mixture to the lemon zest mixture. Strain the mixture, pour into sterilised bottles and seal. Leave in a cold, dark place for seven days before serving.

6 Serve cold and, once opened, store in the fridge.

FERRIGNO APERITIVO
ferrigno family aperitif

This is a wonderful ice-breaking cocktail which my grandfather insisted on serving at all family gatherings. I had it on offer at the launch of my last book!

PER PERSON

2 tbsp Limoncello (see opposite)

Prosecco (a dry sparkling white wine from Venice)

ice

1 lemon slice

a sprig of fresh mint

1 Pour the Limoncello into a large wine glass and top up with Prosecco.

2 Add the ice, lemon slice and mint. Serve at once.

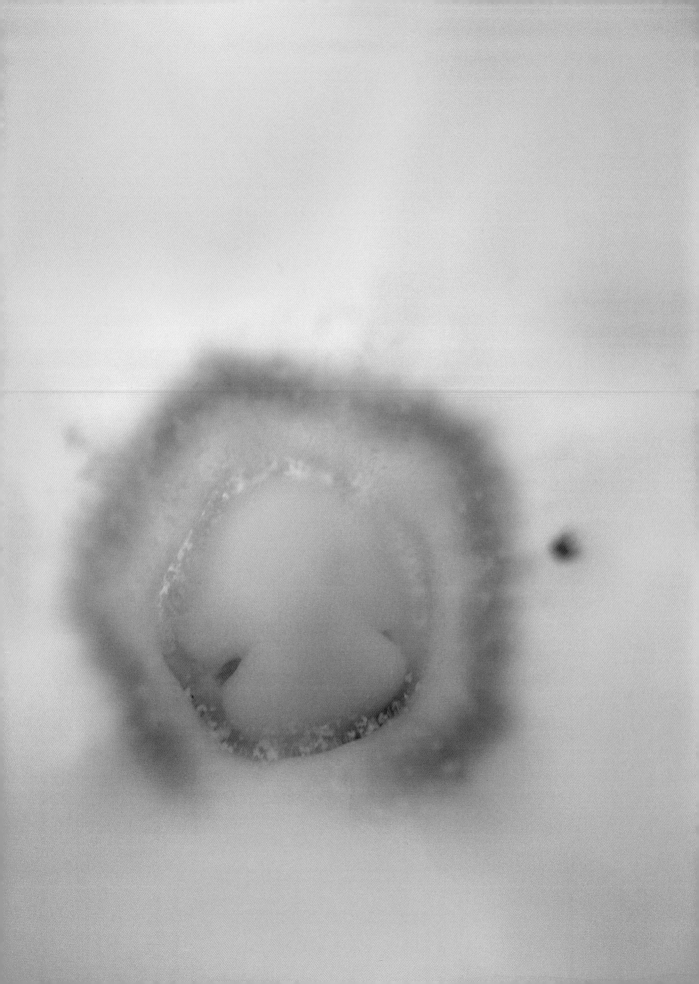

ESTATE

summer

'There from the tree
We'll cherries pluck, and pick the strawberry;
And every day
Go see the wholesome country girls make hay...'

'Bermudas', Andrew Marvell (1621–1678)

ACQUACOTTA
'cooked water' soup

There are many variations of this classical soup, which comes from the Maremma region of southern Tuscany. Curiously enough, my most enduring memory of this soup is of a hot summer's day in a restaurant in Saturnia: after a long day of doing nothing but sit in the sun, the soup was very refreshing and satisfying!

SERVES 6

2 tbsp olive oil

500g (1lb 2oz) white onions, peeled and sliced

2 celery stalks, finely chopped

2 carrots, scrubbed and finely chopped

2 garlic cloves, peeled and crushed

500g (1lb 2oz) fresh plum tomatoes

12 very thin slices firm, coarse-textured bread

1.5 litres (2¾ pints) boiling water

6 large eggs

sea salt and freshly ground black pepper

a handful of fresh flat-leaf parsley leaves, chopped

6 tbsp fruity extra virgin olive oil

1 Heat the oil in a large saucepan and sauté the onion over a moderate heat until translucent. Add the celery, carrot and garlic. Put the tomatoes through a mouli di legume or sieve held directly over the saucepan. Simmer the mixture over a low heat for 20–30 minutes.

2 Meanwhile, toast the slices of bread. Place them in the bottom of the soup tureen. Add boiling water to the tomato mixture, then the eggs one at a time, so that they poach. Season with salt and pepper, and simmer for seven to 10 minutes.

3 Pour the soup over the bread slices in the tureen; let stand for five minutes to allow the bread to absorb the flavours. Serve hot sprinkled with parsley and drizzled with oil.

POMODORO

tomatoes originated in Peru and Ecuador, and had been domesticated and were growing in Mexico long before the Spanish arrived in South America. It's amazing that they were regarded with suspicion for so long: perhaps it was because they are related to deadly nightshade. The name 'tomato' in fact is derived, through the Spanish 'tomate', from the Aztec 'tomatl'. In Britain and France the fruit was known as the 'love apple' (pomme d'amour) and in Italy as 'pomodoro' – 'golden apple' – because the first varieties in Europe were yellow. The Spanish brought tomatoes to Europe in the sixteenth century, and Gerard's Herbal of 1597 records the distrust accorded the fruit in the colder north: 'In Spaine and those hot Regions they use to eate the Apples prepared and boiled with pepper, salt, and oyle: but they yeeld very little nourishment to the body, and the same naught and corrupt'! It was not until much later that tomatoes were taken seriously as food, particularly in southern Italy.

POMODORI RIPIENI DI RISO
tomatoes stuffed with rice

Tomatoes filled with rice are one of the most popular summer dishes in Rome. They may be eaten hot, but most often are served cold. The important thing is to use tomatoes that are very ripe and not watery and use lots of herbs to flavour them. In particular use oregano.

SERVES 6

6 good sized ripe tomatoes

85g (3oz) Arborio rice, cooked

a handful of fresh oregano

a handful of fresh marjoram

a handful of fresh mint

a handful of fresh parsley

60ml (2fl oz) olive oil

2 garlic cloves, crushed

sea salt & freshly ground black pepper

extra virgin olive oil, to serve

a little freshly grated Parmesan, to serve

1 Cut a slice from the top of each tomato to make a cap. Carefully hollow out the tomato and sieve the flesh into a bowl.

2 Add the rice, herbs, oil, garlic, salt and pepper and let stand for 30 minutes to blend all the flavours.

3 Meanwhile sprinkle the insides of the tomatoes with salt and turn upside down to drain out the moisture.

4 Preheat the oven to 180°C / 350°F / gas mark 4. Drain the rice, reserving the tomato liquid. Fill the tomatoes with rice and pour a little tomato liquid on top of each.

5 Replace the caps and arrange in a baking dish. Bake for one hour or until the rice is tender, adding the reserved tomato liquid as it is absorbed.

6 Serve with a drizzle of fruity extra virgin olive oil and Parmesan cheese.

SALSA DI POMODORINI
cherry tomato salsa

Pomodorini are small tomatoes that are extra sweet and very delicious. However, if you find that they are slightly over-ripe, this sauce is the perfect way of using them up. In the true south of Italy, the pomodorini are harvested and dried on the vine, hanging up in the eaves above the kitchen. They look like shrivelled cherries. Their concentrated sweet flavours are then used in dishes that require long slow cooking and in soups.

SERVES 4

600g (1lb 5oz) cherry tomatoes on the vine

1 small white onion, peeled and finely chopped

1 tbsp chopped mixed fresh herbs (basil, oregano, parsley, thyme)

4 tbsp fruity extra virgin olive oil

sea salt and freshly ground black pepper

1 Cut the tomatoes in half crosswise, then spoon out the seeds and discard. Coarsely chop the tomatoes and transfer to a small bowl.

2 Add the onion to the tomatoes, along with the herbs, olive oil, salt and pepper.

3 Toss and let sit for 10 minutes. Serve with bruschetta or crusty bread.

ZUCCHINI
courgettes

Zucchini are almost as popular in Italy as tomatoes, and there are a host of recipes making use of them. Although now specifically bred for their small, tender vegetable fruits, and for their flowers, courgettes are actually immature marrows, and if left to grow, would develop to marrow size. Squashes, pumpkins and cucumbers are also related, belonging to a family that originated in the New World, and thus were unknown in Europe until after the sixteenth century. In fact, apart from in Italy, where the major development of the vegetable took place, the courgette was not known widely until at least the nineteenth century. In Britain it was not until the 1950s, when Elizabeth David published her cookery books extolling the cuisine of the Mediterranean, that courgettes started to become familiar.

In Italy, however, they have always been enormously popular, and they are grown all over the country. We braise them, sauté them, stuff them, deep-fry them for fritto misto, and bake them with sauce, besciamella or tomato. Italian courgettes come in all shapes and sizes, and in colours varying from deep green to yellow. Always buy them at about 15cm (6in) long, when they will be tender and flavourful; the skin should be taut and shiny, never wrinkled. Larger courgettes will be watery and may need to be 'degorged' – sprinkled with salt to get rid of excess liquid (although this tends to make the flesh a little flabby). Tiny courgettes, such as those often sold attached to courgette flowers, will be a little tasteless as they have not had time to develop properly. Using courgette flowers is a fairly recent – and delicious – phenomenon. You can buy them in markets and greengrocers in Britain, although they wilt very quickly (revive them in a bowl of iced water), but the best thing is to grow them yourself. Even one plant will supply you with enough flowers, over an all too brief season, for several wonderful taste treats. They are delicious stuffed, or on pizzas and in salads.

ZUCCHINI CON AGLIO E MENTA
baked courgettes with mint and garlic

Courgettes mean the beginning of summer for me, and I always relish the numerous ways in which they can be cooked. Always choose young, tender courgettes. I treat them with the utmost respect, just like aubergines.

SERVES 4

500g (1lb 2oz) medium-sized courgettes, trimmed

a handful of fresh mint leaves, chopped

a handful of fresh flat-leaf parsley leaves, chopped

2 garlic cloves, peeled and crushed

200g (7oz) dried white breadcrumbs

6 tbsp olive oil

125g (4½oz) Parmesan, freshly grated

sea salt and freshly ground black pepper

1 Cut the courgettes in half lengthwise. Scoop out and discard the soft seeds inside. Sprinkle the courgette halves lightly with salt then place them on a wooden board, cut side down. This will let some of the liquid drain away.

2 Preheat the oven to 180°C / 350°F / gas mark 4.

3 Put the chopped herbs in a bowl with the garlic, breadcrumbs and cheese. Add half the oil while mixing with a fork. Season with a little salt and pepper.

4 Oil a shallow baking dish large enough to hold all the courgette halves in a single layer. Wipe the courgettes to remove the excess liquid and lay them in the dish cut side up. Spoon a little of the herb mixture over each half, and drizzle a little oil over the halves. Cover the dish with foil, and bake for 15 minutes. Remove the foil and continue baking until the courgettes are tender and crisp for about 10 minutes, depending on size.

5 Drizzle the courgettes with a little oil as they come out of the oven. Serve warm or at room temperature as part of your antipasto selection.

ZUCCHINI AL FORNO
baked stuffed courgettes

As a cookery teacher, I'm always asked about gluts of fruit and vegetables. Tomatoes may come first in this category, but supplies of courgettes, because they grow so readily (so long as they have some warmth), can also spiral out of control. This recipe is a simple, but very delicious, way of enjoying courgettes at the height of their season.

SERVES 4

3 tbsp olive oil

2 tbsp Italian 00 plain flour

4 medium-sized courgettes, trimmed and cut into thick sticks

1 white onion, peeled and finely chopped

1 garlic clove, peeled and crushed

1 x 400g (14oz) can Italian plum tomatoes

a handful of fresh mint leaves, finely chopped

a handful of fresh flat-leaf parsley leaves, finely chopped

juice of 1 lemon

2 tbsp dried white breadcrumbs

2 tbsp freshly grated Parmesan cheese

sea salt and freshly grated black pepper

1 Preheat the oven to 200°C / 400°F / gas mark 6 and lightly grease a gratin dish with 1 tbsp of the olive oil.

2 Put the flour in a shallow bowl and season it well. Dust the courgette sticks lightly with the seasoned flour.

3 In a large sauté pan, heat another 1 tbsp of the olive oil over a moderate heat and sauté the courgette sticks until lightly browned. Remove from the pan and set aside.

4 Put the remaining oil in the pan and sauté the onion then add the garlic, stir in the tomatoes, mint and half the parsley and bring to a simmer. Adjust the seasoning. Remove from the heat.

5 Put half the cooked courgette sticks in the bottom of the gratin dish and sprinkle with half of the lemon juice. Spoon the tomato mixture over this layer and then cover with the remaining courgettes. Press the layers down. Drizzle with the remaining lemon juice, then sprinkle the top of the mixture with breadcrumbs and Parmesan. Season with salt and pepper.

6 Bake in the preheated oven for 20 minutes until golden brown. Sprinkle with the remaining parsley to serve.

FIORI DI ZUCCA RIPIENI
courgette flowers stuffed with mozzarella and anchovies

My love of courgette flowers developed when, as a child, I was learning about cookery from my grandmother in the south of Italy. They can be eaten in a variety of ways, but this recipe is a more recent example, encountered in Rome, as a topping for the famous pizza bianca. I hope that courgette flowers will become as popular in Britain as they are in Italy, because they are delicious!

SERVES 6

16 large courgette flowers

8 salted anchovies, rinsed and filleted

85g (3oz) fresh mozzarella cheese cut into 16 cubes

3 large eggs, beaten

100g (3½oz) fine dried breadcrumbs

olive oil

sea salt and freshly ground black pepper

1 Remove the stems and stamens from the flowers. Rinse them under cold water and pat dry with paper towels.

2 Stuff each flower with an anchovy fillet and a cube of mozzarella. Twist the top of the flower to seal and close it. Dip in the beaten egg then coat with breadcrumbs.

3 Heat 2.5cm (1in) oil in a large frying pan. When the oil is hot add the blossoms, a few at a time. Fry until they are golden. Remove with a slotted spoon and drain on kitchen paper.

4 Sprinkle with salt and pepper and eat immediately.

VERMICELLI CON ZUCCHINI
vermicelli with courgettes

If possible, try to find romanesco courgettes for this recipe. These have deep ridges along their length and are thinner and drier than ordinary courgettes. They are crunchy rather than juicy, and intensely flavoured. They are readily available in Italy, and I hope they might soon become more familiar in Britain. You could buy some seed in Italy, the next time you are there, and grow them at home, as they will grow easily here in Britain.

SERVES 6

150ml (¼ pint) olive oil

1kg (2¼lb) medium-sized courgettes

115g (4oz) Parmesan cheese, freshly grated

115g (4oz) sweet Provolone, freshly grated

55g (2oz) unsalted butter, cut into little pieces

a handful of fresh basil and mint leaves, torn

sea salt and freshly ground black pepper

500g (1lb 2oz) vermicelli

1 Heat the oil in a deep frying pan. Cut the courgettes into thin slices and fry a few at a time in the hot oil until lightly golden. Remove and place in a large bowl.

2 Add the two cheeses, butter, basil, mint, salt and pepper.

3 Cook the vermicelli in plenty of boiling salted water until al dente. Drain thoroughly and return to the saucepan in which it was cooked, together with the courgette mixture. If necessary, add a few spoonfuls of olive oil. Mix with the courgettes over a low heat, until the butter and cheese melt to form an emulsion or sauce. Serve immediately.

PEPPERONI

peppers

Peperoni or capsicums belong to the Solanaceae family, along with the potato, tomato and deadly nightshade (and tobacco!). They are native to tropical America and the West Indies, and were not known in the West until after the great explorations and discoveries of the sixteenth century. The pepper family includes not only the large sweet, mild peppers now so familiar to us, but literally hundreds of varieties of hot chilli peppers. Originally we could only get green peppers in the UK and then red peppers, which are ripe versions of the green ones, but new strains with vivid and surprising colours have been developed: you can find yellow, orange, white, even 'black',

and in Holland I've seen lilac ones. They come in a variety of shapes as well, although the 'bell' shape is still the most common. Look for shiny, plump, unwrinkled specimens and avoid any that have soft spots. They should feel heavy, which means that the flesh is thick.

In Italy, we eat them raw in salads or with pinzimonio (olive oil dip) and bagna cauda (hot garlic and anchovy sauce), stuffed and baked, fried, pickled and braised with tomatoes and onions for peperonata, the Italian version of ratatouille. I particularly like them roasted, skinned and served as an antipasto or they can be puréed after roasting (or grilling) and skinning for a pasta sauce.

PEPERONATA ALLA CAMPAGNOLA

country style peppers

This is a classic pepper dish from the south of Italy, where peppers grow in profusion. I should think that every household has its own 'blend'. Some peperonata in a jar with good olive oil to cover makes a wonderful present to give to friends – the essence of summer!

SERVES 4

6 tbsp olive oil

1 red onion, peeled and sliced

2 garlic cloves, peeled and sliced

2 large red and 2 large yellow peppers, deseeded and cut into strips

sea salt and freshly ground black pepper

350g (12oz) plum tomatoes, skinned and chopped

350g (12oz) new potatoes (such as the Nicola variety), peeled and cubed

1 fresh red chilli, deseeded and finely chopped

a handful of fresh flat-leaf parsley leaves, finely chopped

a handful of fresh oregano leaves, finely chopped

1 Heat the oil in a heavy pan, add the onion and garlic and cook gently for five minutes.

2 Add the peppers and salt and pepper. Cook for a further five minutes, stirring occasionally.

3 Add the tomatoes, potatoes, chilli, parsley and oregano to the peppers. Adjust the seasoning to taste, cover and simmer for 20–30 minutes, stirring frequently until thickened. Serve hot or cold as an antipasto.

CRESCENTA DI MOZZARELLA E PEPERONI

pastry crescents with mozzarella and roasted peppers

I first tasted these pastry circles in an enotteca in Florence, when lunching with my mother. We saw them being made and assembled, and we just couldn't wait to get our hands on them. I think we ate more than we should have done...

SERVES 4

Crescenta:

225g (8oz) Italian 00 plain flour

a pinch of sea salt

a pinch of bicarbonate of soda

125ml (4fl oz) whole milk

olive oil for frying

Dressing:

125ml (4fl oz) fruity extra virgin olive oil

1 shallot, peeled and finely chopped

6 marinated anchovies, chopped

175ml (6fl oz) dry white wine

1 garlic clove, peeled and finely chopped

a handful of fresh basil leaves, torn

1 To prepare the crescenta: knead the flour, salt, bicarbonate of soda and milk to a dough, being careful not to overwork it (about 10 minutes). Wrap and leave for an hour. Break off a small golf ball-sized piece of dough and roll out into a very thin disc, 18cm (7in) in diameter. Repeat with the rest of the dough. You should have 16 discs.

2 Fry the discs one at a time in plenty of olive oil, shaking the pan vigorously until the dough circles aerate and become crisp and golden. Drain on kitchen paper and sprinkle with sea salt. Keep warm until ready to serve.

3 To prepare the dressing: heat the oil very gently in a small pan. Add the shallot and sweat until soft. Add the anchovy fillets, white wine, garlic and basil and gently heat through.

4 Blend the anchovy mixture in a food processor until smooth, then pass through a fine sieve. Season to taste.

5 Meanwhile, preheat the oven to 200°C / 400°F / gas mark 6, to prepare the peppers for the topping. Put a roasting tray in to heat up.

Topping:

2 large red peppers

sea salt and freshly ground black pepper

a large handful of wild rocket leaves

125ml (4fl oz) fruity extra virgin olive oil

4 x 100g (3½oz) balls of buffalo mozzarella

12 marinated anchovy fillets, left whole

6 Add a little olive oil to the hot roasting tray. When the oil is hot, add the whole peppers and cook in the hot oven for five minutes until blistered all over. Sprinkle with salt. Remove from the heat, place in a bowl and cover. Once the peppers are cool, skin and de-seed them carefully, then cut each pepper into six large strips.

7 To assemble the dish: toss the rocket leaves in a little oil. Tear each mozzarella ball into three pieces.

8 Place a piece of mozzarella on each crescenta, then arrange the anchovy fillets and roasted pepper strips on top. Scatter over the rocket leaves with a little salt.

9 Spoon the dressing over and around the crescente and finish with a light drizzle of extra virgin olive oil.

FAGIOLINI DI SANT'ANNA
green beans in garlic sauce

When I'm writing and running short of recipes, my friend Anna from Perugia helps me out, and this is one of her recipes – simple, straightforward and delicious. You could ring the changes with a handful of toasted pine kernels scattered on at the end, or alternatively you could include cooked new potatoes. A tbsp of fresh oregano added towards the end of the cooking would be good as well.

SERVES 4

3 tbsp olive oil

2 garlic cloves, peeled and crushed

1 large ripe tomato, skinned and chopped

550g (1¼lb) green beans, topped, tailed and cut in half

100g (3½oz) cooked new potatoes, halved (optional)

sea salt and freshly ground black pepper

1 Heat the oil in a medium saucepan, add the garlic and fry gently until coloured. Stir in the tomato then add the beans and potatoes (if using).

2 Add enough water to barely cover the beans, then season to taste and bring to the boil. Lower the heat, cover and simmer for 15–20 minutes until the beans are tender.

3 Remove the lid and increase the heat towards the end of the cooking time to reduce the juices. Serve hot or cold.

FAGIOLINI VERDI

green beans, like so many vegetables with which we are now so familiar came from America (the only native European bean was the broad bean). Beans fall into many categories, but here we are talking about green beans, the ones that may be eaten pods and all (French beans, runner beans etc.). The pods may be large or small, flat or cylindrical, and are usually green, but in Italy can be yellow, blue, purple or green streaked with purple. The pods should be plucked when young for maximum tenderness, before the internal beans can start to mature and grow. The pods should be bright in colour and 'snap' when broken in two. Some pods need to be 'stringed', the runner particularly, but most French type beans only need topping and tailing. The beans are then dropped into boiling water. Whether or not this should be salted is a matter of argument. Some Italian experts consider that the salt is best added towards the end of boiling, which should be fast and uncovered (to preserve the wonderful colour). Beans cook in five to 10 minutes on average, depending on size. This depends, of course, on whether you like beans well cooked or al dente, still a little crisp.

MACCHERONI CON PISELLI
macaroni with fresh peas

This particular dish is neither soup nor primo piatto, 'starter'. It falls into a category of its own – my grandmother's cooking. It celebrates the best of what you have – i.e. fresh peas, good potatoes and good pasta – and makes for very simple and satisfying eating.

SERVES 6

1 medium onion, peeled and finely chopped

2 garlic cloves, peeled and crushed

1 tbsp olive oil

2 tbsp canned Italian plum tomatoes

1.2 litres (2 pints) water or vegetable broth (see page 128)

500g (1lb 2oz) podded fresh peas

4 new potatoes, peeled and cut into medium chunks

a handful of fresh flat-leaf parsley leaves

sea salt and freshly ground black pepper

300g (10½oz) macaroni

freshly grated Parmesan cheese

a handful of fresh basil leaves, torn

1 Sauté the onion and garlic in the oil for a few minutes until soft. Add the tomatoes and water or stock, bring to the boil and simmer for a few more minutes.

2 Add the rest of the ingredients, except for the pasta, cheese and basil, and season to taste. When the potatoes and peas are nearly cooked, after about 10 minutes, add the macaroni. Cook until al dente.

3 Taste for seasoning, then serve with plenty of Parmesan cheese, basil and black pepper.

PISELLI

peas probably originated in Asia, and they have been used as food since ancient times. We are most familiar with the garden pea, which is eaten green out of the pod, but field peas were once grown for the mature seeds which were only eaten dried, as a pulse. Nowadays we have developed peas with edible pods, known as sugar-snap or mange-tout; the pods of these lack an inner

tough and fibrous layer. In Italy the pea season is short – May into June (later in Britain) – and during this time they virtually provide daily fare. As young broad beans are available at the same time, we might often have broad beans for lunch and a vast dish of peas for supper. The very first peas, however, are eaten raw with bread and salt and a glass of wine.

GRANA
PADA
STAGIONATO
MINIMO UN K.
A ETTI
RMIGIANO
REGGIANO
STRAVECCHIO
£28900

BIETOLE RIPIENE
stuffed swiss chard (from apulia)

Italians love creating dishes with green foods, especially in the south. Swiss chard, which is becoming more commonly available now, can be used not just as a vegetable, but as a 'container' or 'carrier' for other ingredients and flavours. This recipe is a prime example.

SERVES 4

unsalted butter for greasing

450g (1lb) small, tender Swiss chard leaves, well washed

300g (10½oz) ricotta cheese

1 large egg, lightly beaten

55g (2oz) Parmesan, freshly grated

a handful of fresh flat-leaf parsley leaves, finely chopped

sea salt and freshly ground black pepper

BIETOLA

swiss chard is a member of the beet family, along with spinach. It looks rather like a large dark green cos lettuce, but has thick, fleshy white (or red) stalks. The leaves, when removed from the stalks, can be cooked like spinach; they do not wilt as much as spinach, and they are coarser in texture and flavour. The stalks need to be cooked separately, chopped into pieces, in boiling salted water, then eaten in salads or baked with a sauce.

1 Preheat the oven to 200°C / 400°F / gas mark 6. Butter a 33 x 23cm (13 x 9in) baking or roasting tin.

2 Trim off the stalks from the 12 largest leaves (keep for another dish). Fill a pan with three litres (5¼ pints) water and bring to the boil. Add salt to taste and the leaves and boil until the leaves are soft. Transfer the leaves to a colander, and refresh with cold water. Gently squeeze the leaves to eliminate all the water. Dry on paper towels and set aside.

3 Trim the stalks from the remaining Swiss chard leaves (and keep for another dish).

4 In a bowl, mix the ricotta, egg, 45g (1½oz) of the Parmesan, the parsley, salt and pepper.

5 Spread open the large Swiss chard leaves and arrange them so that the flat side of the centre rib is facing up. Mound equal amounts of the filling 1cm (½in) from the end of each leaf. Fold the sides in to cover the filling. Roll the leaves towards the stem end.

6 Arrange the stuffed Swiss chard leaves seam side down, in the prepared tin. Sprinkle with the remaining Parmesan, cover with foil, and bake in the preheated oven for 20–30 minutes. Serve hot.

MISTICANZA
sautéed mixed greens

This particular dish illustrates the importance of greens, which form a fundamental part of Italian eating served as contorne – as a vegetable – throughout the summer season. Tossing the greens in the pan with chilli and garlic – saltata in padella – makes them more interesting. And you could then add some fresh lemon juice at the end.

SERVES 4

675g (1½lb) mixed greens (spinach, Swiss chard, purple sprouting broccoli, endive)

sea salt and freshly ground black pepper

2 tbsp olive oil

2 garlic cloves, peeled and crushed

1–2 small hot chillies, deseeded and finely chopped

extra virgin olive oil

1 Trim and thoroughly wash the leaves and vegetables.

2 Fill a large pan with three litres (5¼ pints) water and bring it to the boil. Add salt to taste. Stir in the greens and boil for three to five minutes, or until just tender. Drain and refresh under cold water and drain again. Squeeze to eliminate all of the water, then coarsely chop.

3 Heat the olive oil in a large sauté pan over a medium heat. Add the garlic and chillies and cook lightly to soften. Add the greens, and sauté until heated through. Season with salt and pepper. To serve, sprinkle with good extra virgin olive oil.

CANNELLONI CON FAVE E RICOTTA

cannelloni with broad beans and ricotta

The combination of pasta and beans – a double carbohydrate – is truly delicious and nutritious. The subtle colours and flavours make this a very special dinner party dish, and something to look forward to during the all too brief broad bean season.

SERVES 6

Pasta:

150g (5oz) Italian 00 plain flour

150g (5oz) fine semolina

a pinch of sea salt

2 large free-range eggs

1 tbsp olive oil

Filling:

1kg (2lb 4oz) broad beans in the pod, podded

350g (12oz) ricotta

110g (4oz) Pecorino Romano, grated

1 large garlic clove, crushed

a large handful of mint, chopped

sea salt and freshly ground black pepper

extra grated Pecorino to serve

Bechamela sauce:

600ml (1 pint) milk

2 slices onion

1 bay leaf

1 blade mace

3 parsley stalks, bruised

5 whole black peppercorns

150ml (¼ pint) white wine

55g (2oz) butter

40g (1½oz) flour

sea salt and freshly ground black pepper

1 To make the pasta: heap the flour and the semolina into a mound on the work surface. Sprinkle over the salt and mix well. Hollow out a well in the centre and break in the eggs. Add the olive oil and, with much care and patience, gradually work the eggs and oil into the flour until you have a slab of dough. Shape this into a ball and leave under a towel or in clingfilm to rest while you prepare the filling.

2 To make the filling: boil or steam the broad beans until tender, about 10 minutes. Drain and leave to cool. Once cool, put half of the beans in a food processor and pulse, leaving some texture. Add the ricotta, Pecorino, garlic, mint and salt and pepper to taste. Add the remainder of the whole broad beans and mix well with a wooden spoon.

3 Roll out the pasta dough wafer thin and cut into squares of 8 x 8cm (3 x 3in). Sprinkle lightly with semolina and let dry on a tray for 10–15 minutes. Once almost dry, cook the pasta squares in boiling, salted water. Drain when cooked but still firm to the bite.

4 Preheat the oven to 200°C / 400°F / gas mark 6.

5 To make the bechamela: place the milk in a pan with the onion slices, bay leaf, mace, parsley stalks and peppercorns. Heat over a medium–low heat and bring to a simmer, remove from the heat and leave to infuse for eight to 10 minutes.

6 Melt 25g (1oz) butter in a saucepan and stir in the flour; stir over the heat for one minute, remove from the heat and strain in the infused milk and mix well. Return the saucepan to the heat and stir or whisk continuously until boiling. Add the remaining butter and wine and simmer for three minutes. Season with salt and pepper to taste.

7 On each pasta square spread 1 tbsp of the broad bean filling and roll up into a cylinder. In a casserole or baking dish, spread half of the bechamela sauce, place the filled cannelloni and layer with the remaining bechamela. Sprinkle with extra grated Pecorino cheese and bake in the preheated oven for 15 minutes. Serve immediately.

FAVE

broad beans were the only beans known in Europe before Columbus discovered America, and brought back varieties of green beans. The time to enjoy broad beans is May to early July. When the pods are young, pale green with a satiny bloom, and the beans inside are small and not fully mature, the pods may be quickly boiled or steamed and eaten whole. A village tradition in Italy is to shell young broad beans then eat them raw with Pecorino cheese. As the season progresses, the pods become thicker, longer and coarser, and the inner beans develop quite a tough, fairly indigestible outer skin. This is when you should cook the podded beans lightly, then remove the outer skin to reveal bright green and tender morsels. The classic herb to serve with broad beans is mint (indeed the two are often grown together as mint helps keep blackfly away).

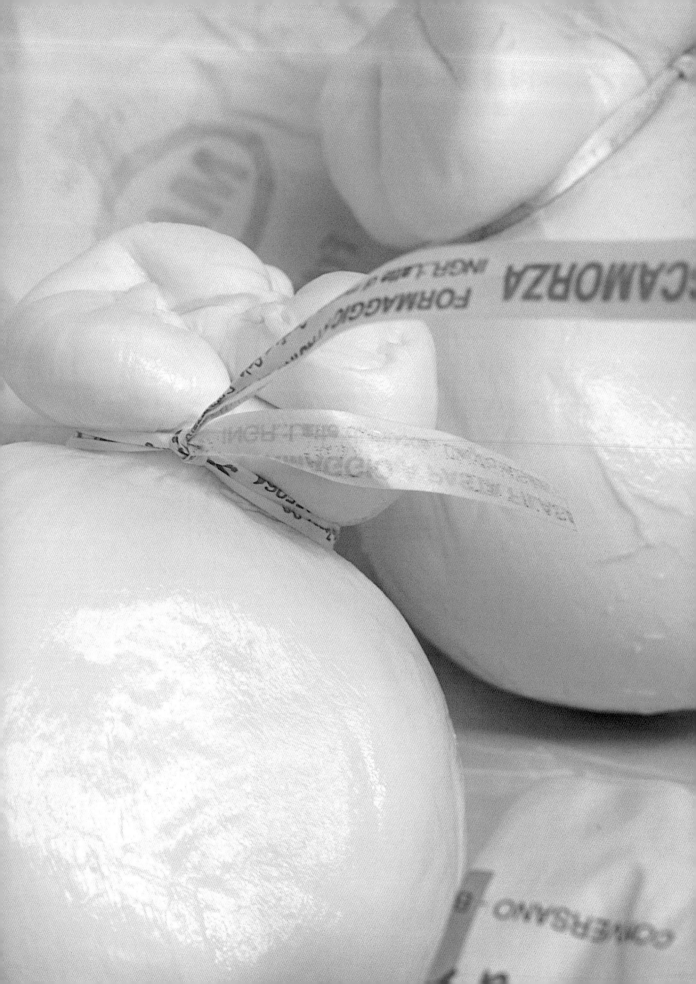

MOZZARELLA DI BUFALA

buffalo mozzarella cheese

In the terraced houses that line the winding streets of Naples, and in farm kitchens all over the rugged southern parts of Campania with its fertile volcanic soil, mozzarella has long been a staple part of the local diet. No-one knows exactly how long the cheese has been made in the south of Italy, but as early as 60 AD the Romans are recorded as making a similar food, curdling fresh milk with rennet extracted from the stomach of a sheep or goat. Legend also has it that the monks of San Lorenzo de Capua gave bread and 'mozza' cheese to the hungry who came begging in the third century. Eventually this cheese reputedly made by the monks became known as 'mozzarella' (the word deriving from the Italian verb mozzare, to cut off, the action of breaking the cheese curd into smaller, more manageable portions).

The transition of mozzarella made from sheeps' milk to what is now considered the real thing – made from the creamy milk of buffaloes – came about many centuries afterwards. Indian water buffaloes, which roam wild in south-eastern Asia, were first introduced to Campania and other areas of southern Italy in the sixteenth century. They thrived in the mild, dry climate, producing a rich, white milk which was transformed into a creamy mozzarella di bufala.

Today there are still some small family cheese makers that produce mozzarella in much the same way as then. As daylight breaks over the gentle hills of Campania, buffalo milk from provincial farms is distributed among cheese makers in Naples and the surrounding countryside, who make fresh mozzarella from it daily. It is poured into large aluminium tanks, allowing 4.5 litres (7¾ pints) of milk for every kilogram (2¼lb) of the finished cheese. The milk is heated and a coagulant added to form the curd. Once this has formed it needs to be broken up into smaller pieces, with excess liquid cheese being drained away to form the delicious mozzarella. The firm cheese that remains is heated and kneaded until it achieves just the right elasticity.

Mozzarella is best eaten fresh, drizzled with the finest extra virgin olive oil, sea salt and black pepper, and accompanied by sweet, ripe tomatoes. Nothing could be more delicious, but there are a few more ideas in the following pages, which will ably demonstrate the cheese's versatility.

SOFFIATINI

pancakes stuffed with spinach and mozzarella

These pancakes come from Piacenza in Emilia, and no matter how many times I make them, they are always welcomed by my friends and guests. In fact, it's a very useful dish altogether. One of its main merits is that it can be cooked in advance and reheated when needed – a great boon when we are all so busy.

SERVES 4

Filling:

85g (3oz) unsalted butter

85g (3oz) Italian 00 plain flour

200ml (7fl oz) whole milk

115g (4oz) cooked spinach, chopped

a pinch of sea salt

freshly ground black pepper

a pinch of freshly grated nutmeg

115g (4oz) mozzarella, diced

55g (2oz) Parmesan, freshly grated

2 egg whites, whisked

sea salt and freshly ground black pepper

Pancakes:

90g (3¼oz) Italian 00 plain flour

150ml (¼ pint) whole milk

2 large eggs, beaten

a pinch of sea salt

85g (3oz) unsalted butter, melted

freshly grated Parmesan

1 To make the filling, melt the butter in a saucepan, add the flour and cook for one minute to make a roux. Slowly add the milk, stirring all the time; cook over a moderate heat, stirring constantly, until the sauce has thickened. Add the spinach with a pinch of salt and cook for a further minute. Fold in the remaining ingredients and leave to cool.

2 Preheat the oven to 180°C / 350°F / gas mark 4.

3 To make the pancakes, mix the flour and milk in a saucepan. Add the eggs and a pinch of salt and whisk. Pass the batter through a sieve. Brush a 30cm (12in) round, heavy frying pan with melted butter and set over a moderate heat. Pour a small ladleful of the pancake batter into the pan and make a thin pancake. Repeat with the remaining butter and batter, to make four pancakes. When cooked on both sides, stack each pancake on a plate.

4 Put a spoonful of the filling in the centre of each pancake and fold over two edges to meet in the centre, then fold over the other two edges making a parcel.

5 Place on a greased, high-sided baking tray. Brush with the remaining melted butter and sprinkle with Parmesanto taste. Bake in the pre-heated oven for 10–15 minutes. Serve immediately.

TORTA TARANTINA
potato and mozzarella cake

This recipe comes from Taranto, a region in Puglia, which is famous for its rich soil, and thus its really good potatoes. There are many rules in Italian cooking, one of them being that fish and cheese should never be eaten together (we would not serve Parmesan on a fish pasta or risotto, for instance). It is only with pizzas and in this dish that you will find that forbidden combination – mozzarella and anchovies.

SERVES 6

1kg (2¼lb) Italian new potatoes (Spunta are good)

1 x 225g (8oz) can Italian plum tomatoes, chopped

olive oil

2 garlic cloves, peeled and crushed

320g (11oz) mozzarella, sliced

8 marinated anchovy fillets, chopped

1 tsp dried oregano

sea salt and freshly ground black pepper

1 Boil the potatoes in their skins in salted water until tender. Place the tomatoes in a colander and allow to drain for 10–15 minutes to rid them of as much moisture as possible.

2 Preheat the oven to 200°C / 400°F / gas mark 6.

3 Skin the potatoes and force through a *mouli di legume*. Add salt and pepper to taste, 1 tbsp of olive oil and the crushed garlic.

4 Oil a round pizza tray and spread the potato mixture over it. Arrange the mozzarella slices on the potato layer and scatter the anchovies on top.

5 Arrange the tomatoes over the potatoes and anchovies, sprinkle with the oregano and drizzle another tbsp of olive oil over. Bake for 20 minutes in the preheated oven. Serve hot.

STROMBOLI
rocket pesto and mozzarella loaf

Several years ago, I was teaching Italian cooking on a cruise ship in the Mediterranean. Late one night, as we were eating dinner, the captain announced that if we looked to starboard we would see the volcano Stromboli in eruption. I was very excited as I had been making this bread for many years, and it was the first time I had been introduced to its namesake! The bread acquired its name because during baking the cheese bursts out from its confining bread crust, looking a little like molten lava...

SERVES ABOUT 8

Biga starter:

2.5g (⅒oz) fresh yeast

150ml (¼ pint) warm water (blood temperature)

125g (4½oz) strong white flour

Dough:

10g (¼oz) fresh yeast

175ml (6fl oz) warm water (blood temperature)

1½ tsp salt

375g (13oz) strong white flour

3 tbsp olive oil

Rocket pesto:

3 tbsp pine kernels, toasted

2–3 garlic cloves, peeled

finely grated zest of 1 lemon

1 large bunch of rocket, about 100g (3½oz) in weight

approx 100ml (3½fl oz) olive oil

sea salt

55g (2oz) Parmesan, finely grated

1 To make the biga starter: dissolve the fresh yeast in the water. Add the flour and mix to a smooth, thick batter. Cover and leave to ferment at room temperature for 12–36 hours until loose and bubbling.

2 To make the dough: dissolve the fresh yeast in half of the water. In a large bowl, mix the salt and into the flour. Make a well in the centre.

3 Pour in the yeast mixture, olive oil and biga and combine. Add the remaining water and mix to form a soft, sticky dough, adding extra water if necessary.

4 Turn the dough out on to a floured surface and knead until smooth, silky and elastic, about 10 minutes. Place dough in a clean oiled bowl, cover and leave to rise until doubled in size, about one and a half to two hours.

5 Meanwhile, make the pesto: process the pine kernels and garlic until finely chopped.

6 Add the lemon zest, rocket and a third of the olive oil, and process until the required texture is achieved, gradually adding more oil.

Filling and topping:

125g (4oz) rocket pesto (see p92)

300g (10oz) mozzarella

olive oil

sea salt

fresh rosemary sprigs

7 Stir in the Parmesan by hand and season with salt. Adjust the olive oil content to reach desired consistency – this pesto needs to be quite thick. Cover and chill. (It's good with *gnocchi* and pasta).

8 Preheat the oven to 180°C / 350°F / gas mark 4.

9 Knock the dough back and chafe (a rotating, shaping motion), then rest for 10 minutes.

10 Roll the dough out into a rectangle approximately 35 x 20cm (14 x 8in).

11 For the filling: smother the dough in rocket pesto. Tear the mozzarella into cubes and lay evenly over the pesto.

12 Roll the dough up like a Swiss roll, starting at one of the shorter sides. Do not roll too tightly. Place on an oiled baking sheet and pierce the rolled dough in several places with a knife or skewer.

13 Sprinkle with olive oil, sea salt and rosemary leaves, and then bake in a preheated oven for 45 minutes or until golden brown.

14 Remove the loaf from the oven, cool slightly, then and sprinkle with additional olive oil.

CAPONATA DI NAPOLI
bread and mozzarella salad

During the book's photo shoot, Jason Lowe, the photographer, queried this recipe, thinking that we couldn't possibly include something so mundane as a bread salad. But how wrong he was. I assembled the dish and, after many protests, he agreed to shoot it. Then he proceeded to devour the whole lot – and asked for more! It may be deceptively simple, but it's vital that you use the best possible ingredients. (You could also add garlic, capers or olives if you liked.)

SERVES 4

450g (1lb) slightly dry, firm-textured, country-style bread

4 ripe tomatoes, de-seeded and diced

450g (1lb) mozzarella, torn into 1cm (½in) pieces

a handful of fresh basil leaves, torn

1 tsp dried oregano

125ml (4fl oz) bold, fruity extra virgin olive oil

sea salt and freshly ground black pepper

1 Tear the bread into small chunks. Combine with the tomatoes, mozzarella, basil, oregano and salt and pepper to taste.

2 Drizzle generously with olive oil. Mix well and serve.

GNOCCATA AL POMODORO
semolina pizza

The semolina gnocchi base of this dish from Emilia-Romagna is wonderfully light, like clouds, and to me represents the ultimate comfort food. It's also a great store-cupboard recipe because, more often than not, everything is to hand in the kitchen. I've made it several times for friends who, after an initial reluctance (for it doesn't sound very promising), were fully converted.

SERVES 4

1.5 litres (2¾ pints) whole milk

sea salt & freshly ground black pepper

375g (13oz) fine semolina

3 large eggs

85g (3oz) Parmesan, freshly grated

3 tbsp olive oil

1 x 225g (8oz) chopped Italian plum tomatoes, drained

300g (10½oz) mozzarella thinly sliced

2 tbsp fine dry breadcrumbs

a handful of fresh oregano leaves, chopped

1 Preheat the oven to 200°C / 400°F / gas mark 6. Bring the milk to the boil with a little salt. Sprinkle the semolina over the surface stirring all the time and cook for 20 minutes. Let cool to lukewarm.

2 Beat the eggs with a little salt and pepper and add to the semolina with the grated cheese and mix well.

3 Coat a large round pizza tray with some of the oil. Turn the semolina mixture onto it and cover with the drained tomatoes. Arrange the mozzarella slices on top and dust with the breadcrumbs and oregano.

4 Sprinkle with the remaining oil. Bake for 20 minutes and serve.

PARMIGIANO REGGIANO

parmesan cheese comes from a small specified area around the rivers Po and Reno in north-central Italy. Made with semi-skimmed, unpasteurised cows' milk, the cheese is straw-coloured with a brittle, grainy texture and a fruity, fragrant flavour. The thick, hard brown rind is stamped 'Parmigiano Reggiano', which is the guarantee of origin. A good aged cheese is recognisable by its salt crystals, which in Italy we call 'snowflakes'. They should be marbled throughout the cheese.

At one or two years old, Parmesan is pale, supple and crumbly. At this stage it is good for use in desserts, especially with pears, apples, grapes or nuts. It is also served grated into olive oil, as a dressing. At three or four years it is darker, drier and very hard, and is the classic grating cheese for pasta, risottos and other dishes.

GNOCCHI ALLA ROMANA
roman-style gnocchi

This recipe typifies the Roman style of eating, using a gnocchi mixture in a more refined, decorative way. The Romans enjoy this in the winter months usually, but it should not be reserved for then, as it's good all year round. It makes a great lunch in the summer with bread, wine and lots of salad.

SERVES 4

1.5 litres (2¾ pints) whole milk

1 tsp freshly grated nutmeg

375g (13oz) fine semolina

3 large egg yolks

85g (3oz) unsalted butter

85g (3oz) Parmesan, freshly grated

1 Bring the milk to the boil with the nutmeg in a large saucepan. Add the semolina all at once, stirring rapidly so that no lumps form. Cook over a low heat for about 20 minutes, still stirring, or until the mixture comes away easily from the sides of the pan. Remove from the heat and let cool a little.

2 Add the egg yolks to the semolina one at a time, then half the butter and half the Parmesan.

3 Turn the semolina out onto a board and spread it into a circle about 5mm (¼in) thick. Smooth the surface with a spatula dipped in cold water and let it cool completely. Cut the semolina into 5cm (2in) circles using a glass.

4 Preheat the oven to 200°C / 400°F / gas mark 6, and butter a large baking dish.

5 Arrange the gnocchi in a single layer in the buttered dish, slightly overlapping. Melt the remaining butter and pour it over the gnocchi. Sprinkle with the remaining Parmesan. Bake until golden brown, about 20 minutes. Serve hot.

GELATO DI RISO
rice ice-cream

The texture of the rice gives this ice-cream body and substance. This is a particular favourite of mine, and I first enjoyed it at a famous gelateria in Rome. You might be alarmed by the inclusion of the ground rice, but please try it, you will be amazed. You can serve the ice-cream with seasonal fruit or a chocolate sauce. It's good to give to children who are not eating, as it contains some good protein and carbohydrate.

SERVES 4

250g (9oz) ground rice

a pinch of sea salt

finely grated zest of 2 unwaxed lemons

1 litre (1¾ pints) whole milk

8 large eggs, separated

300g (10½oz) caster sugar

500g (1lb 2oz) mascarpone

about 2 tsp vanilla extract

250g (9oz) amaretti biscuits, crushed

1 Put the ground rice in a saucepan with the salt, lemon zest and milk.

2 Cook over a low heat for 25 minutes, stirring occasionally, until the mixture is thick and smooth. Leave until cold.

3 Beat the egg yolks with the sugar until pale and creamy. Add the mascarpone cheese and mix thoroughly.

4 Whisk the egg whites until peaks form, then add the vanilla. Fold the mascarpone mixture into the egg whites gently but thoroughly. Fold in the rice mixture with the crushed amaretti.

5 Pour into a shallow freezer container and freeze or put into an ice-cream machine and churn. In a freezer, it will take two hours.

MASCARPONE

mascarpone is exclusively Italian. A soft cream cheese, it is made from cows' milk, and comes from Lombardy. It has a rich, butter-coloured paste, a silky smooth texture, and a luscious, light, whipped-cream taste. In parts of Italy it is eaten fresh as a dessert – often with fruit and a sprinkling of sugar – or flavoured with espresso, chocolate or liqueur. It is also the main ingredient of the famous Venetian tiramisù, a creamy dessert which will 'pick-you-up'. In Italy, the best mascarpone is enjoyed from September to October, using summer milk, but the cheese is now available all year round.

BASILICO
basil

Basil, a labiate annual plant with white flowers and tender, light green leaves, is extremely variable. The leaves may be small or large, but this herb is always recognisable by its smell, which is intensely aromatic, rather like sweet cloves. Basil is one of the best herbs to grow at home, but it is actually a warm country plant, preferring a sunny location; native to India, in temperate climates it is better started in a heated greenhouse. I always bring my basil seeds from Italy. There are two varieties worth growing: lattuga, which is lettuce-leaf basil (its leaves are enormous, about half your hand size), and genovese, which has very small leaves. Lattuga is ideal for adding to

sauces towards the end of their cooking. Genovese, which is also known as basilico nano or 'dwarf basil', is used to make pesto sauce and is added to tomato preserves.

All basil leaves are best when picked before the spike of flowers is out, and should be eaten as soon as possible. Cutting off the flower spikes will encourage the growth of new side shoots. Unlike tougher herbs, basil does not dry well, but you can preserve your home-grown basil during the winter months by layering it with sea salt in a dark jar with a dark lid in the fridge. This way it will remain perfect and will be far less expensive than the supermarket plants that have so little flavour.

POLPETTE DI MELANZANE CON POMODORO AL FORNO

aubergine patties with roast cherry tomatoes

These ostensibly meaty patties are ideal for vegetarians, and taste divine. Use as much basil as you like, or you could of course substitute flat-leaf parsley. Serve the polpette and tomatoes on a bed of wild rocket, with some extra basil if you like.

SERVES 6

Polpette:

2 medium aubergines, finely diced

sea salt and coarsely ground black pepper

3 tbsp olive oil

zest of 2 unwaxed lemons

2 large eggs, beaten

75g (2¾oz) Parmesan, freshly grated

30g (1¼oz) Pecorino, freshly grated

200g (7oz) mozzarella, cut into tiny dice

300g (10½oz) fine dried breadcrumbs

100g (3½oz) pine kernels, roughly chopped

a generous handful of fresh basil leaves, finely chopped

2 garlic cloves, peeled and finely chopped

Roast tomatoes:

200g (7oz) cherry tomatoes (preferably pomodorini)

1 garlic clove, peeled and finely chopped

2 tsp clear honey

zest of 2 unwaxed lemons

2 tbsp olive oil

1 Put the aubergine into a colander, mix in 2 tsp salt, and leave for 20 minutes. Rinse well and squeeze dry.

2 Heat the olive oil in a large frying pan and stir-fry the aubergine, in batches if necessary.

3 Preheat the oven to 200°C / 400°F / gas mark 6.

4 In a large bowl, mix all the remaining ingredients for the polpette into the fried aubergine. Season with salt and pepper, then form the mixture into walnut-sized balls. Arrange these on an oiled baking tray.

5 Halve the cherry tomatoes, and spread them on a separate baking tray. Scatter with all their seasonings, as well as some salt and pepper.

6 Cook the polpette on a shelf above the tomatoes for 10–15 minutes, until golden brown. The tomatoes should roast in about the same time. Serve hot.

SALVIA

sage is derived from the Latin salvus or 'healthy', referring to its therapeutic properties. It was used by the Egyptians, Romans and Greeks; the latter considered it to be sacred and offered it to the gods. Sage grows wild in the Mediterranean basin from the shore line up to elevations of about 750m (2,500ft), preferring sunny arid scrubland, rich in limestone. It does not like wind. There are several hundred types of sage. The plant is perennial, with shoots of pale grey-green long oval leaves growing in bunches that cover the woody branches underneath. In Italy sage is used in many dishes. Leaves are added to the butter in which calf's liver is fried, or to dried beans that are being braised. Leaves are deep-fried in a batter in Tuscany.

SALVIA FRITTA
fried stuffed sage leaves

This is what I would call a very impromptu dish – you wander into the garden, stop by the sage bush, then pick, press and fry! It's wonderful as an antipasto, and delicious with a glass of dry sparkling Prosecco. Try to use the smallest leaves, as they are more intensely flavoured.

SERVES 4

32 fresh sage leaves

8 salted anchovy fillets, rinsed and dried

2 large eggs

olive oil for frying

1 Place 18 sage leaves face up on a baking sheet. Cut anchovy fillets lengthwise in half. Top each leaf with an anchovy half. Cover each anchovy with a sage leaf face down and press the leaves together. Place a baking sheet over the leaves and top it with weights for 15 minutes.

2 Lightly beat the eggs and add the leaves. Heat 1cm (½in) oil in a frying pan over a medium heat. When hot, lift the leaves one at a time out of the bowl and let excess egg drip back in. Fry the leaves until golden, turning once. Drain the leaves on paper towels and cook all the others in the same way.

POMODORI SECCHI CON ORIGANO

preserved tomatoes with oregano

Tomatoes can become a problem in Italy, as we have too many, which all seem to become ripe at the same time. This recipe bring back a rash of childhood memories, of opening up the larder at home and seeing row upon row of scarlet jars, brimming with tomatoes ready to be enjoyed later in the year. They are a perfect antipasto dish, and really delicious with bread as a panini (sandwich), which we used to have when we came home from school. The preserved tomatoes represent a ready-made cheese and tomato sandwich filling!

SERVES 4

2kg (4½lb) good plum tomatoes

6 garlic cloves, or more to taste, peeled and finely chopped

4 dried chillies (peperoncino), or more to taste

a generous handful of fresh oregano leaves

250g (9oz) Pecorino cheese, freshly grated

extra virgin olive oil

ORIGANO

o r e g a n o was given the name 'splendour of the mountains' by the Greeks. At least 60 species exist, many of which grow wild in Sicily, choosing rocky and arid fields, coastal areas and mountains, so long as it is sunny. The most fragrant oregano grows high up in the mountains, where the night cold preserves the fragrance much better than the shoreline heat. Oregano is more pungent dried than fresh. For the strongest flavour, pick oregano as soon as the plant is in bloom, then hang a bunch in the shade until dry, and then in the sun until brittle (or put it in a very low oven). Crush the oregano between the palms of your hands over paper. Sift, then put in a glass jar and tightly close.

1 Preheat the oven to 140°C / 275°F / gas mark 1.

2 Pour water into a pan large enough to hold all the tomatoes at the same time, and bring to the boil. Add the tomatoes when the water is boiling. Just a couple of minutes is enough to soften the skins slightly.

3 Drain the tomatoes, then cut them in half and spread out on a baking sheet. Place in the preheated oven for 40 minutes – or let them dry in the sun!

4 In the meantime, prepare a seasoning by mixing together the garlic, peperoncino, oregano and grated Pecorino.

5 Take one tomato half at a time and dip the inner side in the seasoning mixture. Put two halves together, kissing like a sandwich, and place on the bottom of a sterilised jar, one after the other, until you reach the top. Cover with extra virgin olive oil, close tightly, and store in a cool place.

SARDE A BECCAFICO
stuffed sardines

This peasant dish, found only in Sicily, combines sardines and orange, an unusual but tasty mix of flavours. The boned sardines are rolled around a stuffing and then are baked with the tails sticking up, which makes them look like beccafichi, little birds!

SERVES 6

1kg (2¼lb) fresh sardines

55g (2oz) currants

6 tbsp olive oil

100g (3½oz) dried white breadcrumbs

55g (2oz) pine kernels

2 garlic cloves, peeled and finely chopped

a handful of fresh flat-leaf parsley leaves, chopped

sea salt and freshly ground black pepper

12 bay leaves

juice of 2 oranges

juice of 1 lemon

1 tsp caster sugar

SARDINE

sardines and pilchards are available separately in cans in Britain, because we think they are two different types of fish, but in reality they are one and the same. Sardines are simply a smaller version of the pilchard. Fresh sardines are caught in the Mediterranean, and I love them, finding them extremely versatile, grilled, baked, stuffed, filleted and 'melted' into a sauce. They are also very good in marinated dishes, so can be cooked ahead of time.

1 Cut the heads and fins off the sardines, but not the tails. Slit the belly and clean out the guts. Place the fish on a board, open side down, and press gently down on the backbone. Cut the backbone at the tail end and remove it. Wash and dry the fish.

2 Meanwhile, put the currants in a bowl and cover with warm water. Let them plump up for 10 minutes. Drain and dry on kitchen paper.

3 Heat half of the oil in a frying pan and fry the breadcrumbs until golden. Mix in the pine kernels, garlic, parsley and currants. Sauté for a few minutes, then remove the pan from the heat. Add salt and pepper to taste.

4 Preheat the oven to 180°C / 350°F / gas mark 4.

5 Sprinkle the sardines on both sides with a little salt and pepper. Place, skin side down, on the work surface. Spoon a heaped teaspoon of stuffing over each fish and roll up towards the tail. Place in a suitable baking dish with the tails sticking up.

6 Stick the bay leaves here and there amongst the little bundles. Drizzle the orange and lemon juices, the remaining olive oil and the sugar over the fish.

7 Bake in the preheated oven for 20 minutes. Serve at room temperature.

CALAMARI IN TEGLIA
baked squid with potatoes

SERVES 4

Squid:

12 medium squid, 10–13cm (4–5in) long, with tentacles, cleaned

1 medium onion, peeled and sliced 5mm (¼in) thick

2 garlic cloves, peeled and crushed

2 large plum tomatoes, peeled, de-seeded and chopped

a handful of fresh flat-leaf parsley leaves, finely chopped

450g (1lb) Italian potatoes, such as the Spunta variety, peeled and sliced 1cm (½in) thick

1 dried chilli (peperoncino), coarsely chopped

4 tbsp of olive oil

Stuffing:

150g (5½oz) dry country-style bread, crusts discarded, torn into small pieces

2 large eggs, beaten

1 garlic clove, peeled and crushed

a handful of fresh flat-leaf parsley leaves, peeled and chopped

sea salt and freshly ground black pepper

1 To make the stuffing: soak the bread in a small bowl of warm water for five minutes. Drain and squeeze dry. Mix the bread with the eggs, garlic and parsley, then season with salt and pepper.

2 Stuff the squid with the stuffing mixture, filling them halfway only, as the stuffing will expand when cooked. Seal the open end of the squid with toothpicks.

3 Arrange the onion, garlic, tomatoes and parsley in a 3 litre (5¼ pint) round flameproof terracotta casserole at least 22cm (8½in) in diameter, or a cast-iron pot. Season with salt and pepper. Pour 3 tbsp of water into the casserole, cover with the potato slices slightly overlapping, and sprinkle with the chilli.

4 Arrange the squid and the tentacles on top. Drizzle with olive oil. Cover and simmer slowly over a low heat for one hour. Check the casserole to be sure it remains on a slow simmer.

CALAMARI

s q u i d are cephalopods, as are cuttlefish and octopus. They are torpedo-shaped with eight arms and two tentacles, and vary in size from a few centimetres long to science-fiction giants, which are amongst the most formidable of deep-sea predators. Those caught in the Mediterranean – by lure and lights, at night – are small to medium in size, and are very

popular in Italy. Once cleaned (which is simpler than many people believe), the body sac can be stuffed and fried or baked, perhaps using the chopped arms and tentacles as part of the stuffing; the sac can also be sliced into rings and deep-fried in batter as part of a fishy fritto misto. Squid can also be stewed.

INSALATA DI BOTTARGA
bottarga salad

SERVES 4

1 x 5cm (2in) bottarga (grey mullet), sliced very thinly

8 cherry tomatoes, halved

1 celery heart, finely chopped

3 tbsp fruity olive oil

freshly ground black pepper

1 Mix all the ingredients well together, and that's it!

BOTTARGA

Nearly every Mediterranean region offers some version of bottarga, born of the need to preserve fish eggs. The solution? Salting the egg sacs, pressing them under heavy weights to draw out the moisture, and drying them. Once dried, the salami-like logs can be kept for months. Tuna and grey mullet are the most common. Tuna bottarga is more common in Sicily, while the Sardinians prefer grey mullet bottarga. That made from grey mullet eggs comes packed in wax, so be sure you remove this with a paring knife before you start slicing or grating the bottarga.

Bottarga was an ancient Egyptian delicacy, and it is still very popular there today. It can be served as a merenda or snack with drinks, alone or with oil and lemon juice, freshly ground black pepper and parsley. It is also served grated with pasta or rice. The flavour is very strong and salty, so it must be grated, or very finely shaved or sliced.

MACCHERONI ALLA BOTTARGA DI FAVIGNANA
macaroni with bottarga

I first tested this recipe on my family, but then I know their tastes so well. It's always a little daunting to try something like this on strangers, especially as the flavours, so typical of southern Italy, are very strong. However, the recipe has proved to be a great success, I'm glad to say! The pine kernel 'cream' in particular has drawn comments, as it makes a very pungent and rich topping/garnish.

SERVES 4

3 garlic cloves

25g (1oz) pine kernels, preferably Italian

2 tbsp olive oil

10 cherry tomatoes (pomodorini), halved

1 tbsp dry white wine

300g (10oz) macaroni

sea salt

a handful of fresh flat-leaf parsley leaves, chopped

2 tbsp extra virgin olive oil

100g (3½oz) bottarga di tonno (pressed tuna roe), chopped very finely

1 In a pestle and mortar, crush two of the garlic cloves and the pine kernels to a cream. Keep aside.

2 Pour the olive oil in to a medium-sized saucepan and heat. Add the remaining garlic clove, sliced, the tomatoes and the wine. Stir-fry for three minutes until the wine has been absorbed.

3 Cook the pasta in boiling salted water until al dente, then, drain and toss with the sauce, parsley, extra virgin olive oil and the bottarga.

4 Top with the pine kernel cream and serve immediately.

FRUTTI DI MARE IN UMIDO
mixed seafood casserole

In Britain we are extremely fortunate to have excellent quality seafood, and we have recently learned to enjoy it more, thanks to the efforts of writers and restaurateurs like Rick Stein. He has demystified the whole world of seafood for us. One of the primary wonders of seafood is that it is so quick and simple to cook, and it is very nutritious – facts long known to the Italians. Here is a perfect example, a very typical Ligurian casserole.

SERVES 4

24 mussels

24 clams (Venus variety if possible)

8 slices dry white country bread

4 tbsp olive oil

3 garlic cloves, peeled and crushed

3 plum tomatoes, de-seeded and chopped

a handful of fresh flat-leaf parsley leaves

350ml (12fl oz) dry white wine

COZZE E VONGOLE

mussels & clams are good value because the shells are much thinner than those of many other shellfish, so that pound for pound there is more meat in them. They can either be kept for a day in a bucket of lightly salted water or bought for immediate consumption. Clean them under cold running water, scrubbing off any sand or mud; tug off the 'beard', the tuft which protrudes from the hinge. If any mussels remain open after this, discard them because they are certainly dead and may be toxic. Clam flesh is firmer than that of an oyster or mussel, and you need to prepare and cook them carefully. Scrub well under cold running water then, to open, place in a lidded saucepan and stew just until they open. Always buy, cook and eat clams the same day.

1 Preheat the oven to 200°C / 400°F / gas mark 6.

2 Prepare the shellfish. Remove the beards from the mussels, and scrub the shells. Wash the clams thoroughly. Discard any clams or mussels that do not close (they may be dead).

3 Arrange the bread slices in a single layer on a baking sheet and toast them in the preheated oven for six minutes. Turn the slices and toast for six minutes more. Transfer to a wire rack to cool completely.

4 Heat the olive oil in a large sauté pan over a medium heat. Add the garlic and cook gently until the garlic has softened. Add the tomatoes and half the parsley, increase the heat to medium high and cook, stirring constantly, for one minute.

5 Pour in the wine and simmer briskly until half the wine has evaporated. Add the mussels and clams, reduce the heat to medium, cover the pan and cook for about 10–12 minutes, until all the shells have opened. Discard any that have remained closed.

6 Transfer the mixture to a large serving platter, sprinkle with the remaining parsley and arrange the toasted bread around the edge of the platter. Serve immediately.

MELONE

melons were first cultivated on a large scale in Italy, and two varieties are particularly associated with Italy, the napoletano and the cantalupo. When ripe, all melon varieties should yield to slight pressure at the stalk end, and some have an unmistakable melon scent. My benchmark for ripeness is when a melon feels heavy for its weight; this means it has a maximum sugar content. Chilled melon is good for breakfast in Italy, combined with other summer fruits, or as a starter with Parma ham. Take care that melons are well covered if stored in the refrigerator, otherwise they impregnate everything around them with their heavy scent.

SORBETTO DI MELONE
melon sorbet

The sugar used in this recipe can vary according to the sweetness of the melon. During the long hot summers in Italy, when people are prostrate with heat, lying about fanning themselves, a spoonful of melon or melon sorbet can bring them back to life. I once saw an even more unusual usage of melon: on a sizzling beach at midday, a mother put an empty half melon shell on her child's head to cool him down and protect him from the sun!

SERVES 4

2 ripe cantaloupe melons
75–150g (2¾–5½oz) caster sugar

1 Cut the cantaloupes in half and scoop out the seeds. Cut the halves into wedges, remove the skin and cut the flesh into 2.5cm (1in) chunks. Purée in a food processor until smooth. Add sugar to taste, which is a personal matter, starting with 75g (2¾oz).

2 Chill the purée for two hours, then freeze it in a suitable container or churn in an electric ice-cream machine. Store the sorbet in the freezer until ready to serve then scoop into dishes and enjoy.

CROSTATA DI CILIEGIA
cherry tart

Cherries are perhaps at their best in this tart. In the warmth of southern Italy, the tree, once planted, quickly produces its wonderful blossom in spring, followed by the fruit in May and June, rather earlier than in Britain. You can use this tart concept with any of your favourite fruits, as it is a really delicious pastry, flavoured with hazelnuts.

SERVES 6

Pastry:

200g (7oz) Italian 00 plain flour

a pinch of sea salt

150g (5½oz) unsalted butter

85g (3oz) icing sugar

55g (2oz) toasted, shelled and finely chopped hazelnuts

1 large egg yolk

Filling:

700g (1lb 9oz) washed ripe cherries

350g (12oz) mascarpone cheese

25g (1oz) icing sugar

2 tsp vanilla extract

1 tbsp brandy

CILIEGIA

cherries are sharp, sweet and fleshy, with juice that stains the lips, fingers and everything the fruit comes in contact with. They are a summertime treat well worth waiting for. There are two main types: sweet and sour. When shopping for cherries, examine the stems, as these are a good indicator of freshness: they should be green and flexible, not dry and brittle. In Italy cherries are usually eaten fresh, but over the centuries they have been used in sauces, soups, poached with sweet spices or pickled.

1 Sift the flour and salt into a bowl and rub in the butter until the mixture resembles fine breadcrumbs. Stir in the sugar and hazelnuts.

2 Stir in the egg yolk and about 2 tsp of water, and mix to form a dough. Wrap in greaseproof paper and chill for 30 minutes.

3 Meanwhile pit the cherries, and preheat the oven to 190°C / 375°F / gas mark 5.

4 On a lightly floured surface roll out the pastry and use to line a loose-bottomed 28cm (11in) flan tin. Prick the base, line with paper and weight down with baking beans. Bake in the preheated oven for 15 minutes until the sides of the pastry are crisp. Remove the lining and the beans and return to the oven for five minutes until the bottom is crisp. Leave to cool.

5 In a large bowl, combine the mascarpone cheese with the icing sugar, vanilla and brandy. Spoon into the cooked pastry case, smooth the surface then top with the cherries and serve.

TORTA DI CILIEGIA

cherry cake

SERVES 6

115g (4oz) unsalted butter, softened

150g (5½oz) golden caster sugar

4 large eggs, separated

200g (7oz) Italian 00 plain flour

1 tsp baking powder

1 tbsp brandy

a pinch of sea salt

225g (½lb) cherries, washed and pitted

vanilla icing sugar for dusting

1 Preheat the oven to 180°C / 350°F / gas mark 4. Grease and flour a 20cm (8in) cake tin.

2 Cream the butter and the sugar together until light and fluffy. Beat the egg yolks with a little of the plain flour. Sieve the remaining flour with the baking powder and carefully fold into the creamed mixture with the brandy and egg yolks.

3 Whisk the egg whites with the salt until they stand in stiff peaks. Add 3 tbsp of the whisked egg white to the creamed mixture and mix well. Fold in the remaining egg white with a metal spoon and carefully spoon into the prepared tin.

4 Scatter the prepared cherries over the top of the cake mixture and press them down lightly.

5 Bake for 35–40 minutes until the cake is well risen and firm to the touch.

6 Allow the cake to cool in the tin, then turn out on to a wire rack and dust with vanilla icing sugar.

ZABAGLIONE SEMI FREDDO
frozen zabaglione

I once heard that a Sicilian doctor prescribed zabaglione to expectant mothers, which makes sense as it contains protein-rich egg yolks and Marsala, a fortified wine which is full of iron. This version is frozen, and is a wonderful variation on a classic theme.

SERVES 6

12 large egg yolks

115g (4oz) light brown muscovado sugar

300ml (½ pint) dry Marsala

300ml (½ pint) whipping cream

175g (6oz) fresh seasonal fruits (strawberries, raspberries etc) to serve

2 tbsp toasted chopped hazelnuts, to decorate

1 In a bowl beat the egg yolks together with the sugar until pale and thick. Stir in the Marsala and mix well.

2 Set the bowl on the top of a pan of hot water (don't let the bowl touch the water) and place over a gentle heat. Stir continuously for up to 12 minutes, until the custard begins to thicken. Be patient. Immediately remove from the heat and stand the bottom of the bowl in cold water to stop the cooking, still stirring. Leave to one side to cool.

3 Whip the cream until standing in soft peaks and then fold into the custard. Freeze for 6 hours or churn in an ice-cream machine following the manufacturer's instructions.

FRUTTI DI ESTATE

summer fruits The large, bright red strawberry we know today has developed over the centuries from the tiny wild fragrant fruit that grows all over Europe and other temperate areas. The latter is still to be found growing in the wild (although it is also cultivated), and is highly valued for its warm musty flavour. If you have to wash any strawberry, do so very briefly and before you remove the hulls, otherwise water will get into the fruit and spoil the delicate flavour. Eat strawberries just as they are – I particularly like them with a squeeze of lemon juice. Raspberries are a soft, warm crimson red with velvety flesh, and grow in many temperate parts of Europe, particularly well as far north as Scotland. They are available in June and July, followed by another crop as late as October. I love them on their own or mixed with other soft fruits. They deteriorate quickly, so pick and eat rather than store for any length of time in your fridge (although they open-freeze well). Raspberries make wonderful jams, juice, preserves and sauces.

PIZZA DOLCE
sweet pizza

This is a really delicious take on the pizza. My grandmother used to make it as a merenda, or snack, for after our siesta, and we accompanied it with a strong espresso. The bread base is topped with a creamy layer and then with fresh fruit. It's good for breakfast too! You can use your imagination and add further ingredients – try some grated or shaved chocolate on top and/or some toasted chopped hazelnuts.

MAKES 2–3 PIZZAS

Brioche dough:

20g (¾oz) fresh yeast

175ml (6fl oz) milk, warmed

450g (1lb) strong white flour

4 large eggs and 2 large egg yolks

5 tbsp golden granulated sugar

½ tsp salt

250g (9oz) unsalted butter, at room temperature, in pieces

1 large egg yolk, to glaze

Topping:

200g (7oz) full-fat cream cheese

2 large egg yolks

2–3 drops vanilla extract

1 tbsp caster sugar

250g (9oz) fresh fruits (strawberries, raspberries etc)

Streusel topping:

175g (6oz) soft light brown sugar

25g (1oz) plain flour

50g (2oz) unsalted butter, melted

1 Preheat the oven to 200°C / 400°F / gas mark 6. To make the brioche: cream the yeast in the milk. Mix in 125g (4½oz) of flour to make a sticky 'sponge' or dough. Cover this with the rest of the flour but do not mix it in. Leave, covered, for 45 minutes in a warm place so the sponge bubbles up through the flour.

2 Mix the flour into the sponge. Add the eggs, yolks, sugar and salt and continue mixing until the dough is very elastic. Add the soft butter bit by bit, waiting for it to be absorbed before the next addition. Knead for five minutes till the dough is smooth and elastic.

3 Cover and leave to rise overnight in a fridge. It should triple in size. If necessary, leave to rise further in the morning. Divide dough into two or three pieces, and roll out into flat circles, 5–8mm (¼–⅜in) thick. Cover and leave while preparing toppings.

4 To make the toppings: mix the cheese with the yolks, vanilla and sugar. Combine all the streusel topping ingredients. Cover the brioche with the cream cheese mix and top with fruits, then sprinkle over streusel topping.

5 Glaze any visible brioche dough with the egg yolk glaze, then bake in the preheated oven for 25–30 minutes or until the crust is puffed and golden, and the streusel topping is crunchy.

GELATO AL CIOCCOLATO AMARO
bitter chocolate ice-cream

Eating gelato in Italy is almost a ritual, and it is enjoyed throughout the entire land. I think the ice-cream of Italy is so good because it is not too rich. It's more milky than creamy, so you can eat it without a heavy feeling afterwards. The most popular flavour is undoubtedly chocolate. Whilst in Siena, try the ice-cream from Nannini, an old-established gelateria, also famous for its panforte. The daughter of the family, Gianni Nannini, is a famous pop-star in Italy.

SERVES 8

8 large egg yolks

175g (6oz) golden caster sugar

1 litre (1¾ pints) whole milk

200g (7oz) bitter chocolate (75% cocoa solids), broken into pieces

250g (9oz) cocoa powder (bitter and high quality)

1 Beat the egg yolks and sugar together until very thick.

2 Pour the milk into a saucepan, add the chocolate and cocoa and bring to the boil slowly, stirring constantly to ensure a perfectly blended mixture.

3 Remove from the heat and beat in the egg yolk mixture while the cocoa-flavoured mixture is still hot. Allow to cool.

4 Pour the mixture into a freezerand freeze for two or three hours until beginning to firm up, then whisk thoroughly. If using an ice-cream machine, follow the manufacturer's instructions and churn until ready.

CACAO

cocoa may not be a seasonal food, but any child can tell you that there's nothing like chocolate ice cream on a summer's day. The chocolate drinks that Cortes and his men tasted when they encountered the Aztecs in South America, and which were enjoyed throughout Europe thereafter, would not have tasted like the chocolate and cocoa drinks we know today. For the process by which the fats, or cocoa solids, are extracted from chocolate beans and pods, thereby achieving a powder similar to cocoa, was not invented until the early eighteenth century. The best cocoa I have ever used is from Peter's Teahouse in FlorenceIt is bitter and delicious and dark purple in colour. It will transform all your chocolate recipes, so when in Florence, do go. I buy it also to make a fabulous, rich hot chocolate drink.

CAFFE'

coffee Two species of the small tropical
coffee tree produce the major part of the
world's coffee supply. The best and most widely
cultivated is arabica. I love coffee, and have a
daily caffè fix of a strong, dark and flavoursome
brew. In Italy espresso bars fill and empty at a
phenomenal rate, particularly in the morning
when having a caffè is almost a ritual for every
Italian. You will rarely have a bad coffee in Italy
as the barrista – the man (or woman) in charge
– handles his coffee with great expertise,
tending his machine like an altar. Coffee
becomes an indispensable element of summer
when partnered with zabaglione; together they
create a delicate and aromatic dish, perfectly
reflecting the season's warmth and light.

ZABAGLIONE CON ESPRESSO
coffee zabaglione

This creamy, velvet-smooth dish is one of the most sensual ways to end a meal. Prepare it for
your lover on a hot summer evening.

SERVES 4

4 large egg yolks

2 tbsp golden caster sugar

a pinch of Italian 00 plain flour

2 tbsp freshly made espresso coffee

1 tsp whole milk

50ml (2fl oz) dry Marsala

1 Cover the bottom of a double-boiler with
2.5cm (1in) water. Heat until water simmers.
Combine the egg yolks, sugar and flour in the
top of the double-boiler. Blend with a wire
whisk and put over the simmering water. Beat
constantly. As the sugar dissolves the mixture
becomes runny, then thickens to double cream
consistency, about five minutes.

2 At this point, pour in the espresso, milk
and Marsala. Continue to beat until the
zabaglione becomes thick and fluffy. This
should take five minutes. Rest for 10 minutes.
Then pour into dishes.

AUTUNNO

autumn

'Season of mists and mellow fruitfulness!
Close bosom-friend of the maturing sun;
Conspiring with him how to load and bless
With fruit the vines that round the thatch eaves run;
To bend with apples the mossed cottage-trees,
And fill all fruit with ripeness to the core...'

'To Autumn', John Keats (1795–1821)

BRODO DI VERDURE
vegetable broth

This is fundamental for risottos, soups and sauces. No cook in Italy would consider compromising here. It is the hallmark of culinary excellence.

MAKES ABOUT 1.5 LITRES (2¾ PINTS)

40g (1½oz) unsalted butter

1 tbsp olive oil

3 garlic cloves, peeled and crushed

1 large onion, peeled and coarsely chopped

4 leeks, cleaned and coarsely chopped

2 carrots, peeled and coarsely chopped

2 celery sticks, coarsely chopped

1 fennel bulb, coarsely chopped

a handful of flat-leaf parsley leaves, finely chopped

4 fresh or 2 dried bay leaves

2 sprigs fresh thyme

1 In a large heavy-based saucepan, melt the butter with the oil. Add the garlic and sauté for two minutes then add everything else and cook until softened, stirring continuously.

2 Add 3 litres (5¼ pints) water, bring to just below boiling point, then cover and simmer for an hour.

3 Remove from the heat and leave to cool for one and a half hours. Return the pan to the heat and simmer for 15 minutes. Strain the stock through a sieve and return to the pan. Boil rapidly until reduced by half. Use as needed. Can be kept in the fridge for up to three days.

PORRI

leeks probably originated in the Mediterranean area, growing wild at first, and leeks in the Mediterranean today are still small and tender, quite unlike those monstrous competition specimens you see proudly displayed in northern British garden shows. Leeks are the sweetest of the onion family. When buying, seek out thin young spears without a central hard core; they should be untrimmed, squeaky fresh and with a large proportion of white to green (although the green can be used in the stockpot). Before using leeks, you must clean them properly because, especially after rain, mud splashes on to the leeks and gets down between the individual leaves. After cutting off the root end and most of the dark green top, you should allow fresh cold water to run between the leaves (you may need to slit them open a little). I love leeks in soups and broth, they are the basis of Italian sofrittos, and they are good as the flavouring element in pasta sauces and risottos.

PAPPA CON POMODORO E PORRI
leek and tomato soup

As I've mentioned, we Italians love to make use of every morsel in our kitchens. We always have leftover bread as it goes stale so quickly, and here is a fine example of a straightforward soup, thickened by leftover bread. The use of a sublime oil to finish is essential.

SERVES 6

6 baby leeks, sliced

50ml (2fl oz) olive oil

675g (1½lb) fresh ripe tomatoes

sea salt and freshly ground black pepper

½ tsp dried chilli (peperoncino)

450g (1lb) crusty day-old bread

750ml (1 pint 5fl oz) Vegetable Broth (see page 128)

6 fresh basil leaves

4 tbsp extra virgin olive oil (estate-bottled)

1 Wash the leeks well under cold running water. Drain, then chop them finely.

2 Heat the olive oil in a large saucepan, add the leeks and fry gently for 10 minutes.

3 Meanwhile, purée the tomatoes in a blender or food processor. Add to the leeks. Add salt, pepper and chilli to taste, then simmer for 30 minutes.

4 Cut the bread into small pieces and add to the pan. Mix well and lightly simmer for five minutes. Add the broth, mix well and simmer for a further 10 minutes.

5 Serve the hot soup in individual bowls. Add a basil leaf and some extra virgin olive oil to each serving.

RISOTTO AI PORRI CON NOCI E VINSANTO

leek risotto with nuts and vin santo

This is my variation on a classic Tuscan risotto. Risotto is a great two-pan meal – one for the broth, one for the cooking – and you know it will be ready in about 18–20 minutes. It's good to get the family involved in the constant stirring a risotto requires – perhaps 10 minutes per child or friend! The ingredients here are only a suggestion: please feel free to create your own flavour combinations, although I think the leek and walnuts give a wonderful texture and colour, as well as taste.

SERVES 4

85g (3oz) unsalted butter

3 shallots, thinly sliced

4 young tender leeks, cleaned and finely chopped

1 tsp green peppercorns, crushed in a pestle and mortar

115g (4oz) shelled fresh walnuts, coarsely minced

350g (12oz) carnaroli risotto rice

125ml (4fl oz) vinsanto

1 litre (1¾ pints) Vegetable Broth (see page 128), hot

100g (3½oz) Parmesan, freshly grated

sea salt and freshly ground black pepper

a handful of fresh flat-leaf parsley leaves, chopped

1 Melt 55g (2oz) of the butter in a large saucepan and sauté the shallots and leeks until translucent. Add the green peppercorns and walnuts and fry for one minute.

2 Add the rice and fry until it becomes golden. Then pour about three-quarters of the vinsanto over the rice and simmer until it is absorbed. Add the warm stock, ladle by ladle, stirring all the time; this will take about 15–18 minutes, never adding more until the last ladle has been absorbed. Then add the remaining vinsanto and cook until the rice is al dente.

3 Turn off the heat and stir in the Parmesan and remaining butter. Season to taste. Let the mixture stand for two minutes with the lid on. It must be all'onda – like the waves. Serve at once sprinkled with the chopped parsley.

MELANZANA
aubergines

Although botanically a fruit, aubergine is usually treated as a vegetable. It belongs to the same family as the potato, tomato and sweet pepper, the Solanaceae. The plant originated in India, was introduced to Spain in the eighth century by the Arabs, and thence to other parts of the world. It is grown in warm temperate countries and the tropics as a field crop; in cooler climates, it has to be cultivated under glass. Aubergine is easy to hybridise, and there are now any number of variations in colour, shape and size: there are tiny green, pea-sized aubergines used in Indian and Thai cooking, egg-shaped white fruit (thus the American name of eggplant), and the purple glossy truncheon-like oblongs we are familiar with in Europe. Some Asian varieties have bristly, knobbly skins.

The name aubergine is thought to have derived from the Arabic – which also led to the common modern Indian name of brinjal. The Italian name derives from the Latin mala insana, or 'apple of madness'. This seems a little alarming, but is perhaps due to the plant's relationship with deadly nightshade or belladonna...

We love aubergines in Italy, and use them a lot in cooking. Perhaps the most famous Italian dish is parmigiana di melanzane, baked layers of fried aubergine with tomato sauce, mozzarella and Parmesan. Aubergines are also made into 'meat' balls, polpette (see page oo), which are wonderfully tasty and filling – in fact, aubergine is known as 'poor man's meat' in Italy. They are delicious stewed in the Italian versions of the Provençal ratatouille. They can be stuffed and baked, or preserved.

Aubergines contain bitter juices. To get rid of these, cut or slice the aubergines and salt them for about 20 minutes before rinsing, drying and using. Most writers say that modern varieties have had the bitterness bred out of them, but I have talked to many Italian farmers who say this is not true. So I still salt, and I think they taste much better as a result. Aubergines are also famous for their ability to soak up oil in cooking. The salting helps a little in this process, and sometimes a brief blanching prevents too much oil absorption. Always drain well on kitchen paper to get rid of surplus oil.

CIAMBOTTA
stewed vegetables

This Neapolitan version of ratatouille is an old-fashioned dish, which can be served as an antipasto or as an accompaniment to meat or fish. I've been quite specific about the chopping because I've realised that haphazardness makes the dish look rather ordinary. Cutting more carefully makes it appear a little more elegant, and it can then be served at occasions other than family meals.

SERVES 4

1 small onion, peeled and sliced

50ml (2fl oz) olive oil

2 garlic cloves, peeled and crushed

350g (12oz) new potatoes, peeled and cut into 2 cm (¾in) chunks

450g (1lb) aubergines, peeled and cut into 2.5cm (1in) chunks

1 red pepper, cored, seeded and cut into 4cm (1½in) pieces

1 yellow pepper, cored, seeded and cut into 4cm (1½in) pieces

4 large plum tomatoes, skinned, seeded and chopped

1 tsp dried oregano

a handful of fresh basil leaves, torn

sea salt and freshly ground black pepper

1 Sauté the onion in the olive oil in a medium sauté pan over a medium heat.

2 Add the garlic, potatoes, aubergine and peppers. Increase the heat to high and cook the vegetables, tossing frequently until the vegetables begin to brown. Stir in the tomatoes and oregano.

3 Scatter the basil over the vegetables and season with salt and pepper. Cover the pan and simmer for 30 minutes.

4 Serve hot or at room temperature, with more basil leaves if desired.

MELANZANE SOTT'OLIO
marinated aubergines

My grandmother used to make this in autumn when the aubergines were ripe. I have very fond memories of what we called 'aubergine day'. We would all know that quite soon, at the end of the simple preparation, we would be enjoying aubergine sandwiches – slices of marinated vegetable squashed between two slices of country bread, oily and fragrant. This dish is best when the aubergine has had enough time to completely absorb the marinade. For this reason, start its preparation at least two days in advance.

SERVES 4

2 medium aubergines, 900g (2lb) in weight, peeled

sea salt and freshly ground black pepper

2 tbsp white wine vinegar

approx. 8 tbsp extra virgin olive oil, (good and fruity)

a handful of fresh mint leaves, chopped

2 tsps fresh oregano leaves

4 garlic cloves, peeled and minced

1 Cut the aubergine crosswise into 2cm (¾in) thick slices. Dissolve 2 tbsp salt in a large bowl of water. Place the aubergine slices in the salted water.

2 In a large pan, combine 600ml (1 pint) water and the vinegar and bring to the boil. Drain the aubergine slices in a colander. Add the slices to the water-vinegar mixture and cook for three minutes. Using a slotted spoon, transfer the aubergine slices to kitchen paper, arranging them in a single layer. Cover with another piece of paper and press lightly to absorb the liquid. Repeat each batch using dry pieces of paper. Drain for one hour.

3 Transfer the aubergine slices to a large bowl. Mix together the oil, herbs, garlic and pepper, with more salt to taste. Pour this mixture over the aubergine, adding more oil if necessary to cover. Cover the bowl and let sit for two days if you can before serving.

AGLIO
garlic

Garlic is believed to have been cultivated since antiquity, and the wild plant probably originated in Asia. It was of enormous gastronomic importance to the Ancient Egyptians, and Hippocrates, the 'father of medicine', was aware of its therapeutic properties. Pliny lists sixty-one garlic remedies. In the Middle Ages across Europe the strong aroma of garlic was very useful in covering up the flavours and odours of ingredients that were no longer fresh. That characteristic smell was also put to other uses. It is said that Marshal von Blucken, defeated by Napoleon at Ligny, fell from his horse and was knocked senseless. He was revived with an infusion of garlic and gin, climbed back on his horse, and carried on to take part in the Battle of Waterloo. Garlic has famously been used to ward off the evil eye, and on 1 May in the village of Bonpietu, near the town of Agrigenti, garlic cloves are chewed by locals to repel the devil, who is reputed to pay them a visit on this day each year. It is well known that the devil hates the smell of garlic!

A member of the lily family along with onion and leek, garlic is available all year round. The bulb is made up of single bulblets, cloves wrapped in papery white skin. In spring the plant produces a large spherical flower cluster with small pink-lilac flowers on a long tubular stem. The new season's garlic appears in early summer. These heads are plumper than the garlic we usually see, with a tight skin. As the bulbs dry out towards the autumn, the cloves loosen, the skin becomes more papery, and the flavour becomes stronger. Wild garlic can still be found, growing in wasteland and damp woods; you can identify it by its smell!

As with most aromatic herbs, the flavour of garlic grown in warm climates is stronger. When bruised or cut, garlic releases allicium, the compound responsible for its aroma. The more it is cut, the stronger the flavour. Buy your garlic from the best possible source, or grow it yourself; it's easy to grow, and tastes even better pulled straight from the earth. Store your garlic somewhere cool and dry, and if the cloves develop green centres, remove these are they are bitter.

Garlic is still considered beneficial to health in many ways, and I think it's as important as a regular dose of vitamin C. There are many ways of cooking it, but I like it best roasted in its skin – whole bulbs or cloves – and then squeezed out like toothpaste on to bruschetta or toast. Never ever burn garlic, and never ever use a crusher – garlic is much too great a gift to be treated like that. Instead, finely slice or chop it, and cook it tenderly, as if you are trying to seduce it.

SPAGHETTI CON AGLIO E OLIO
spaghetti with garlic and olive oil

This is a dish that every cook in Italy will make at least once a fortnight – it's rather like the British beans on toast (which I hate). In Italy we have different grades of spaghetti – something that has been creeping on to British grocery shelves. Grade 6 spaghetti is best for this dish: it is medium to fine in thickness, absorbing all the flavour of the sauce, making for a perfect balance.

SERVES 4

a handful of fresh flat-leaf parsley leaves, finely chopped

115g (4oz) Pecorino, finely grated

3 garlic cloves, peeled and crushed

3 tbsp olive oil

½ tsp dried chilli (peperoncino)

375g (13oz) spaghetti

sea salt and freshly ground black pepper

1 Mix together the parsley and cheese.

2 Put the garlic and olive oil in a medium-sized sauté pan and sauté until lightly golden. Turn off the heat and add the peperoncino.

3 Cook the pasta with a little salt until al dente. Drain, reserving a little cooking liquid. Stir the pasta and liquid (2 tsp), into the garlic sauce. Mix in the parsley and cheese, adjust the seasoning and serve at once.

FUNGHI
mushrooms

Mushrooms are fungi, among the most curious, interesting, useful and delicious of foods. Through the ages fungi have been the object of worship and of myth, and have enjoyed an important place in cooking, literature and medicine.

Fungi belong to a particular class of plant life that feeds off living, dead and decaying organic matter. The part of most edible fungi that we see above the ground is actually the fruiting body of the plant. Beneath the surface is a far-reaching network of thread-like filaments – the mycelium – through which the fungus draws its nutrients. There are many thousands of different types of fungus. Only a few are edible, some are actually poisonous and many are simply not worth bothering with. Very few of the edible types are cultivated – many are actually very difficult to cultivate – and some of the most delicious kinds can only be gathered from the wild. In general, fungi of all types favour dark, damp habitats, such as forest floors rich in leaf litter, though each type has its favourite 'host' plant or environment. Chanterelles and porcini or ceps are said to favour beech woods; field mushrooms grow best in meadows where cows or horses have been grazing.

Some fungi can be gathered in spring, such as the morel, but most emerge in the misty months of early autumn before the frosts set in. They should always be picked in the very early morning before flies and other predators and pickers have had a chance to get at them. In Europe mushroom hunting is a major pastime, and people are expert at identifying them, the complete opposite of in Britain. You should never go wild mushroom hunting without a very good identification book – or, preferably, an expert mushroom hunter.

Mushrooms should have a prominent place in our diet. They contain no cholesterol, carbohydrates or fat, but good vegetable protein and valuable vitamins. Fresh mushrooms, once picked or purchased, are best stored in brown bags in a cool larder or at the bottom of the fridge. Many mushrooms dry very well indeed – especially the funghi porcini so beloved in Italy – so you can enjoy them all year round. They need to be soaked for about half an hour in hot water to reconstitute them. Always use this soaking water as it becomes very strong in flavour.

PATATE CON FUNGHI PORCINI
potatoes with mushrooms

Along the side of Italian roads in autumn, you will encounter a host of vendors offering fresh porcini or ceps, all of them invitingly laid out in boxes, and wrapped with fresh forest leaves. I always find it hard to resist, thus this recipe, which is a great example of how to enjoy these particular mushrooms. Watch out, as there can be little grubs in the stems; keep your eyes open and simply remove them – they won't do you any harm anyway!

SERVES 6

500g (1lb 2oz) Italian potatoes (Elvira or Spunta are best)

400g (14oz) fresh porcini mushrooms or a combination of wild mushrooms

5 tbsp olive oil

4–5 garlic cloves, peeled and crushed

a handful of fresh flat-leaf parsley leaves, chopped

sea salt and freshly ground black pepper

1 Preheat the oven to 180°C / 350°F / gas mark 4.

2 Scrub the potatoes, and slice them 3mm (⅛in) thick. Brush the mushrooms to get rid of any clinging dirt, and slice them 3mm (⅛in) thick.

3 Lightly oil a large roasting pan and place a single layer of potatoes in the pan. Top with some mushrooms and sprinkle with garlic, parsley, salt and pepper.

4 Continue layering the ingredients until you finish them. Drizzle with olive oil, then pour into the side of the pan 150ml (¼ pint) of water.

5 Bake in the preheated oven for one hour or until the potatoes are tender and the top is golden brown; If the mixture seems dry, add a little more water. Serve hot.

POLENTA
maize 'porridge'

Polenta now means a 'porridge' made from maize or corn meal, which is yet another of the foods unknown in the West until the great explorations of the sixteenth century. In Roman times, though, 'polenta' was a porridge made from indigenous grains such as barley, and indeed a polenta made from chestnut flour was eaten in northern Italy until fairly recently.

Polenta is still a speciality of northern Italy, and I think it is a wonderful comfort food: it soaks up flavour, and provides great nourishment. The maize meal comes in different grades, and in different colours: a bright corn-yellow is the norm, but there is also a white version. I am a great advocate of coarse polenta which involves long slow cooking of at least 40 minutes, and constant stirring with a mestolo (wooden spoon) to prevent it sticking to the bottom of the pan. Quick-cook versions are nowhere near so flavourful or satisfying.

When the cooked polenta comes away from the sides of the pan, it is poured on to a communal wooden board in the middle of the table and eaten 'wet' and hot, usually with a sauce. It can also be flavoured with butter and cheese. It can be left to go cold and set, when it is sliced and fried or grilled to accompany sauces, as an alternative to bread. This is something northern Italians do when bad weather prevents them getting to the bakery. Polenta can also be served as a sweet dish, and I particularly like it with dark chocolate, hazelnuts and lashings of mascarpone cheese.

It s considered a proof of true friendship for Italians to eat their polenta together from the same board. In fact traditional polenta eating is rather like the Swiss fondue, where you are all eating from the same vessel, dipping and diving in, sharing the sauces. It is community eating, rustic eating at its best – and it looks great!

FUNGHI PORCINI IN UMIDO CON POLENTA

sautéed porcini mushrooms with polenta

In order to enjoy this dish at its best, it is important to use slow-cook polenta. There are many varieties on the market, but they will produce an inferior result – dry, lacking in creaminess, texture and flavour. However, long slow cooking of polenta does take quite a while, about 40 minutes. When I was a child, this was no trouble: as we were four girls, we all took a turn at stirring, so it wasn't really a chore!

SERVES 8

Mushroom sauce:

3 tbsp olive oil

3 garlic cloves, peeled and crushed

500g (1lb 2oz) porcini, peeled and brushed clean mushrooms (ceps) and sliced

a handful of fresh mint leaves, wild if possible, torn

½ x 115g (4oz) can Italian chopped plum tomatoes, with liquid reserved

sea salt and freshly ground black pepper

4 tbsp extra virgin olive oil

Polenta:

2.4 litres (4 pints) cold water

sea salt

500g (1lb 2oz) coarse ground polenta (ie slow-cook polenta)

1 To start the polenta, place the water in a large heavy-based soup pot, and bring to the boil over a medium heat. Add a generous amount of salt.

2 Pour in the polenta through your hands, whisking continuously to prevent lumps, and cook for 40 minutes over a low heat. Stir frequently, using a wooden spoon.

3 For the mushroom sauce: meanwhile prepare the mushrooms. Place the oil in a large frying pan, add the garlic and sauté for one minute. Stir in the mushrooms and mint and cook for five minutes over a low heat.

4 Add the tomatoes along with 2 tbsp of the reserved liquid, plus salt and pepper, and continue to cook for 10 minutes, stirring continually.

5 When the polenta comes away from the sides of the pan, remove it from the heat and distribute between bowls or boards. Top with the mushrooms and a generous amount of extra virgin olive oil. Serve immediately.

POLENTA CON DUE SALSE
polenta with two sauces

It is considered a show of true friendship for Italians to eat their polenta together from the same board.

SERVES 6

Polenta:

1 litre (1¾ pints) Vegetable Broth (see page 128) or water

sea salt and freshly ground black pepper

200g (7oz) coarse polenta (i.e. slow-cook polenta)

2 garlic cloves, peeled and crushed

115g (4oz) unsalted butter

115g (4oz) Parmesan, freshly grated

To serve:

Mushroom sauce (see p146)

Tomato sauce (see p147)

1 For the polenta: in a large saucepan, bring the broth or water plus 1 tsp salt to the boil.

2 Gradually add the polenta, stirring to prevent lumps. Lower the heat and you must continue, with a wooden spoon, stirring constantly until the polenta pulls away fom the sides of the pan.

3 Add the garlic, butter, cheese, and seasoning continue stirring until smooth and glossy. The whole process should take 40 minutes.

4 Meanwhile, make and warm the sauces. Pour your chosen sauce on the polenta. Serve.

SALSA DI FUNGHI
m u s h r o o m   s a u c e

This is a classic sauce, made by every Italian cook. It's good with polenta, pasta, in a risotto or as a layer in a lasagne.

SERVES 4

675g (1½lb) mixed mushrooms (porcini or ceps and field)

1 tbsp olive oil

55g (2oz) unsalted butter

1 small hot red chilli pepper, seeded and chopped

sea salt and freshly ground black pepper

a handful of fresh flat-leaf parsley leaves, chopped

1 Clean the mushrooms by trimming away dry ends, brushing away any soil or grit, and wiping the mushrooms with a damp cloth.

2 Coarsely chop the mushrooms and combine with the oil, butter and chilli in a large saucepan. Season to taste, cover and cook gently for 10–12 minutes. Add the parsley, pour on to the polenta and serve.

SALSA DI POMODORO
tomato sauce

The balance of flavours here – of the onion, garlic and celery – is particularly interesting; the celery creates an interesting texture as well, which complements the softness of the polenta.

SERVES 4

1 small onion, peeled and minced

2 tbsp olive oil

1 garlic clove, peeled and crushed

1 celery stick, minced

a handful of fresh flat-leaf parsley leaves, finely chopped

16 ripe plum tomatoes, diced

sea salt and freshly ground black pepper

a handful of fresh basil leaves, torn

1 Cook the onion in the olive oil until translucent. Add the garlic, celery and parsley over a low heat, mix well and cook until tender, about 20 minutes.

2 Add the tomatoes and season generously with salt and pepper. Place the lid on the pan and simmer until thick, for 20 or so minutes.

3 Adjust the seasoning and add the basil.

FINOCCHIO
fennel

Wild fennel originated in southern Europe, and was probably quite bitter at first, unlike the fennel herb with which we are now familiar, which is sweet. Fennel herb is a perennial plant which can grow as tall as 1.8m (6ft), covering Italian roadsides from June onwards. It has an erect green stalk with thread-like leaves forming a delicate lace. The flower heads are a bright yellow 'umbrella'. The seeds, actually the fruits, are half-moon-shaped and striped, available in the autumn. It is these that flavour the famous Tuscan salami, finocchiona, (a fresh sausage that was one of my grandmother's specialities) biscuits and bread doughs. The fragrance of fennel,

seed and herb, is unique – a slight hint of anise and liquorice, a mixture of aromatic and spicy.

Florence fennel or bulb fennel is a relation of wild and sweet fennel, and was thought to have been developed in Italy in the seventeeth century. A base bulb swells, and is kept white by being earthed up or 'blanched'.

There are two distinct types of bulb: the male is long and thin while the female is plump with hips (and only the female bulbs have fronds which can be used as a herb). In Italy bulb fennel is eaten raw in salads or pinzimonio or bagna cauda, or baked, or fried in a fritto misto.

BUCATINI ALLE SARDE E FINOCCHIO

pasta with sardines and fennel

Bucatini is a thick, hollow version of spaghetti, more like a long macaroni. I think it is best with this sauce which, being rich, clings to the pasta – and the hole in the middle creates an interesting texture in the mouth. The flavours are wonderful, the sardines marrying beautifully with the fennel.

SERVES 6

Sauce:

1 onion, peeled and finely chopped

2 garlic cloves, peeled and crushed

3 tbsp olive oil

a generous handful of wild fennel leaves, blanched, drained and finely chopped

200g (7oz) Tomato sauce (see page 147)

1 dsp currants

100g (3½oz) pine kernels

sea salt

1 tsp dried chilli (peperoncino)

500g (1lb 2oz) fresh sardines, rinsed and filleted

Pasta topping:

100g (3½oz) fresh breadcrumbs

2 tbsp olive oil

2 tbsp Tomato sauce (see page 147)

1 garlic clove, peeled and crushed

a pinch of dried chilli (peperoncino)

a handful of fresh flat-leaf parsley leaves, chopped

375g (13oz) bucatini pasta

1 For the sauce, sauté the onion and the garlic in the olive oil. Add the fennel and tomato sauce, currants, pine kernels, some salt and the peperoncino. Simmer for 30 minutes.

2 Add the sardine fillets and cook for 12 minutes; they will break up while cooking.

3 For the topping, toast the breadcrumbs in a frying pan, mixing in the olive oil, Tomato Sauce, garlic, some salt and the peperoncino. Stir constantly, without burning the breadcrumbs, until they are a nice amber colour and crunchy to the bite. Serve them in a dish sprinkled with the parsley.

4 Cook the bucatini in boiling salted water until al dente. Drain the pasta, reserving a ladle of the cooking water. Pour half of the sauce into the pan. Add the pasta and stir to coat completely. Pour into a serving dish and cover with the rest of the sauce, using the water if needed. Serve immediately with the breadcrumb topping.

RAVIOLINI AL FINOCCHIO CON SALSA DI ZAFFERANO

fennel ravioli with roasted vegetable and saffron sauce

This dish looks very cheerful with its white, red and yellow, and brightens up many a dinner table! The saffron sauce is excellent with other vegetable and pasta dishes, so will make a great addition to your repertoire. I've had it just with tagliatelle, which was delicious, but it is particularly good here, with the fennel pasta. In fact, this is a dish for the true fennel lover, with fennel inside the raviolini as well as in the sauce.

SERVES 6

Pasta:

115g (4oz) Italian plain 00 flour

115g (4oz) semolina flour

2 large eggs

2 tsp fine sea salt

1 tbsp extra virgin olive oil

Filling:

1 small Florence fennel bulb, finely chopped

200g (8oz) ricotta

15g (½oz) pack fresh basil leaves, shredded

55g (2oz) Parmesan, grated

Roasted vegetable and saffron sauce:

2 Florence fennel bulbs, trimmed and sliced

4 small red onions, peeled and cut in wedges

salt and freshly ground black pepper

5 tbsp extra virgin olive oil

1 garlic clove, peeled and finely chopped

2 shallots, peeled and finely chopped

a large pinch of saffron strands

250ml (9fl oz) dry white wine

350g (12oz) mascarpone

fresh basil, flat-leaf parsley and Parmesan shavings, to serve

1 First make the pasta: open all the windows to cool the kitchen, and rinse your hands in cold water. Sift the flours into a mound on a clean work surface and make a well in the centre. Break in the eggs and add the salt and olive oil. Beat the eggs lightly with a fork and draw in the flour without allowing the eggs to escape, until you have a rough-textured dough.

2 Use your hands to bring the rough dough into a smooth ball. Knead the dough on the work surface, adding a little more 00 flour if necessary, for eight to 10 minutes until the dough is silky smooth. Wrap in clingfilm and chill for 20 minutes.

3 Meanwhile, preheat the oven to 190°C / 375°F / gas mark 5 and make the filling. Lightly steam the chopped fennel for five minutes over a pan of simmering water. Allow to cool slightly, then beat with the ricotta cheese, fresh basil and Parmesan. Season to taste.

4 Remove the dough from the fridge – it should now be smooth and marbled. Cut off an eighth of the dough, wrap the rest in plastic film and return to the fridge. Roll out on a lightly floured surface to flatten it slightly – it should measure about 20 x 7cm (8 x 2¾in).

5 Adjust the pasta machine to the thickest setting possible. Sprinkle semolina flour over the rollers to stop the dough sticking. Roll the dough through the machine. Repeat, then move the machine on to the next setting and roll the dough through in a continuous motion twice. Repeat until you reach the second thinnest setting (many experts never put the pasta through the final setting as they find it often tears). Lay the strip on a work surface and leave to rest for eight to 10 minutes. Repeat with the remaining dough working with a similarly sized piece of dough each time.

6 Use a 7.5cm (3in) fluted cutter to cut out about 54 pasta circles. Spoon a scant tsp of the filling into the centre of each circle of dough. Brush the edges with a little water, fold each circle in half and pinch the edges together to seal.

7 Arrange the finished raviolini on a wire rack and leave to dry for at least 15 minutes (if you are not going to use the pasta straight away, transfer to the freezer at this stage – it can be frozen for up to three months). Keep the leftover dough, cut into small pieces and dry with the rest of the pasta. These can be added to soup as a thickener.

8 To make the sauce, place the fennel and onions on a large baking tray and drizzle over 4 tbsp of the oil. Season with salt and pepper and roast for 25 minutes until just beginning to char.

9 Meanwhile, heat the remaining olive oil in a pan and sweat the garlic and shallots for five minutes over a low heat until softened. Stir in the saffron and wine, bring to the boil and simmer until reduced by half.

10 Stir in the mascarpone and beat the mixture until smooth. Cook over a low heat, stirring, for five minutes. The more you cook the sauce, the more yellow it will become as the saffron gradually infuses into the mixture.

11 Bring a large pan of slightly salted water to the boil and add the raviolini. Return to the boil and cook for three to four minutes (frozen pasta will take five to six minutes). Drain and toss with the roasted vegetable and saffron sauce, and serve sprinkled with Parmesan shavings and the fresh herbs.

FINOCCHI AL FORMAGGIO

baked fennel and cheese

Making this dish recently for a group of students, everyone was a little alarmed at my method, as everything seemed to go into the oven very quickly and with very little fuss. The results were good, though, and I think I have made a few converts!

SERVES 6

6 Florence fennel bulbs, 3 male, 3 female

55g (2oz) unsalted butter

115g (4oz) Fontina cheese, freshly grated

freshly grated nutmeg

50ml (2fl oz) milk

sea salt and freshly ground black pepper

1 Preheat the oven to 220°C / 425°F / gas mark 7.

2 Trim the fennel bulbs and discard the tough outer layers.

3 Cut the bulbs into small wedges and cook in a small amount of boiling salted water until crisp-tender. Drain and place in a greased baking dish with a little of the butter.

4 Season the fennel with salt and pepper. Cover with the grated Fontina, sprinkle with nutmeg and pour on the milk.

5 Dot with the remaining butter, then bake in the preheated oven for 10 minutes. Serve hot.

PASTA DELLA FAMIGLIA FERRIGNO

pasta ferrigno

This dish was created for my family. My father grows the radicchio (a life-long project), my sister loves the cheese, my contribution was the fennel, which I adore, and all of us relish pasta. Stracchino is a cheese that comes from the Lombardy region, made from milk from cows that are 'tired' (stracchi) in autumn after a summer of lush grazing.

SERVES 6

2 tbsp olive oil

1 medium onion, peeled and finely chopped

1 small male Florence fennel bulb, finely chopped

1 garlic clove, peeled and finely chopped

300g (10oz) red radicchio heart, finely chopped

2 sprigs of fresh rosemary leaves, finely chopped

sea salt and freshly ground black pepper

150ml (¼ pint) dry red wine

275g (9½oz) mezze penne pasta

300g (10½oz) stracchino

1 Heat the olive oil in a medium-sized saucepan and gently cook the onion until translucent. Add the fennel, garlic, radicchio, rosemary and salt and pepper to taste.

2 Sauté until the fennel is tender and the radicchio has wilted and changed colour. Add the wine and allow to evaporate on a medium heat.

3 Meanwhile, bring a large pan of water to the boil, add salt when the water is ready and cook the pasta as the packet indicates, or until al dente.

4 Add the block of stracchino to the sauce in the block and mix well – it will melt and form a sauce. Adjust the seasoning to taste.

5 Drain the pasta, toss with the sauce and serve immediately.

COTOLETTE DI FINOCCHI
fried fennel

In Piedmont, vegetables such as fennel, artichokes, celery and the white stalks of Swiss chard are often coated in egg and breadcrumbs and fried in butter. I like the fennel best.

SERVES 6

6 Florence fennel bulbs, 3 male, 3 female

2 large eggs

sea salt and freshly ground black pepper

225g (8oz) dried, fine breadcrumbs

85g (3oz) unsalted butter

freshly grated Parmesan (optional)

1 Clean and trim the fennel bulbs and cut them into wedges. Cook in boiling water for 10 minutes, drain and pat dry.

2 Beat the eggs with a pinch of salt and pepper.

3 Dip the fennel wedges in the egg and coat with breadcrumbs, patting so that the crumbs adhere firmly to each piece.

4 Melt the butter in a large frying pan and fry the fennel until the crumbs are golden brown on all sides. Drain on paper and serve with a sprinkling of grated Parmesan cheese if desired.

TORTA ALLA MELA E ROSMARINO
apple and rosemary cake

This is a delicious combination. I first enjoyed it in Venice and think the rosemary gives it a very memorable flavour. The cake is beautifully moist and is best eaten on the day it is made. If you like the flavours, try apple and rosemary in a pie – and the rosemary could also flavour an accompanying custard!

SERVES 8–12

115g (4oz) unsalted butter, plus extra for greasing

350g (12oz) Braeburn or Cox's Orange Pippin apples (about 3)

juice of ½ lemon

4 large eggs

150g (5½oz) caster sugar

150g (5½oz) plain white or Italian 00 plain flour

1 tsp baking powder

a pinch of fine sea salt

1 tsp fresh rosemary leaves, finely chopped

finely grated zest of 1 unwaxed lemon

icing sugar for dusting

ROSMARINO

rosemary is one of the most common wild plants of the Mediterranean, and it is very strongly aromatic. It grows well as far north as southern Britain where, as with so many other herbs of the Mediterranean, it was introduced by the Romans. It is very popular with lamb, and butchers often sell their meat with bunches of rosemary, much as fishmongers do in Britain with parsley. It is also used with fish, and in sweet dishes. Rosemary branches are used to brush olive oil on to meat or fish to be grilled.

1 Preheat the oven to 180°C / 350°F / gas mark 4. Grease a 23cm (9in) round cake tin.

2 Melt the measured butter then set aside to cool. Core, peel and thinly slice the apples. Squeeze over lemon to prevent browning.

3 Put the eggs and sugar in a heat proof bowl, and stand over a saucepan of gently simmering water. The bowl must not touch the water. Whisk for 10–15 minutes until the mixture is thick, pale and leaves a trail when the beaters are lifted. Remove the bowl from the heat and continue whisking until the mixture is cool.

4 Sift the flour, baking powder and salt together. Gently fold half the flour and the rosemary into the whisked eggs and sugar.

5 Slowly trickle the melted butter around the edge of the bowl and gently fold in. Take care not to stir the mixture too heavily or it will lose its air. Fold in the remaining flour and the lemon zest. Lastly, fold in the apples.

6 Pour the cake mixture into the prepared tin. Bake in the centre of the preheated oven for about 40 minutes until a skewer, inserted in the centre, comes out clean. Turn out and leave to cool on a rack. Just before serving, sift icing sugar over the top of the cake.

FIGO

figs are ancient. They probably originated
in western Asia but have been growing for long
enough around the Mediterranean to grow
wild. They belong to the same family as
mulberries and breadfruit, and there are many
wild species. Figs grow in the same climate as
almonds, olives and oranges, but can also grow
in Britain, much further north. They are
unusual in that the flowers are inside the skin
of the fruit, and many varieties of fig trees need
the fruit to be pollinated by a fig wasp. In
Britain figs are parthenocarpic, able to fruit
without being pollinated. There are many
varieties – common figs, Smyrna figs, San Pedro
figs and the wild caprifigs. These vary in colour
and size, and all are ready when soft.

FICHI DI PALERMO CON CIOCCOLATO
palermo figs and chocolate

My friend Claudio calls these fichi 'fig bombs'! I first made them for an event for 'Slow Food', a
movement to preserve the cooking and traditions of Italy. After ten courses, I rather tentatively
served them, believing no-one could manage to eat them. But they disappeared nevertheless!

SERVES 9 (2 EACH)

18 fresh figs

18 blanched almonds, toasted

18 slices candied orange peel

18 slivers best-quality chocolate

200g (7oz) best-quality chocolate, grated

1 Preheat the oven to 180°C / 350°F / gas
mark 4. Make a vertical cut into each of the
figs. Into the cavity put a toasted almond,
a slice of candied orange peel and a sliver
of chocolate.

2 Arrange the figs on a heatproof dish and
bake in the preheated oven for 10–15 minutes.

3 When warmed through, immediately roll
in the grated chocolate. Allow to cool on a
wire rack, then enjoy.

FICHI FARCITI
stuffed figs

The memory of picking figs straight from the trees as a child in Italy gives these fruits a sort of magic for me. I used to run home with armfuls of them, passing hundreds more squashed in the road. There are so many wonderful ways to eat figs, but of all the recipes, this is my favourite.

SERVES 6

12 ripe fresh figs

55g (2oz) walnut halves, freshly shelled if possible, roughly chopped

3 tbsp fragrant honey

3 tbsp vermouth

115g (4oz) mascarpone

115g (4oz) dark chocolate, 75% cocoa solids

1 Preheat the oven to 200°C / 400°F / gas mark 6.

2 Cut a tiny slice off the bottom of each fig so that it will sit upright.

3 Make 2 cuts down through the tops of the figs, about 2.5cm (1in) deep, at right angles and ease the figs open.

4 In a bowl, mix together the walnuts, honey, vermouth and mascarpone. Spoon into the opened out fig cavity. Bake in the pre-heated oven for 10–15 minutes.

5 Meanwhile melt the chocolate in a bowl over a pan of simmering water.

6 To serve, place two figs on each plate, and drizzle with the melted chocolate.

NOCI

nuts

Nuts are the fruits of various types of trees, some temperate, others tropical, most of the nuts encased in a hard, sealed shell. Some 'nuts' are actually seeds – the Brazil nut, for example – and the peanut is a legume. Nuts are a concentrated source of energy, being high in protein, carbohydrate and fat, and, although they are delicious to eat as a snack, it is easy to pile on the calories, so they should be eaten in moderation. Despite their tough appearance, nuts do deteriorate and should not be kept for months on end. Buy nuts in the shell in relatively small quantities, store them in a cool place and use them up within a few weeks. Avoid any with damp, mouldy looking shells, which can be dangerous as they are a possible source of toxins. In general, choose nuts that feel heavy for their size. Nuts that feel light may indicate that the inner kernel has lost its moisture and is withering. Buy nuts out of their shells with even more caution. Keep packets in the fridge, and use up as soon as you can.

Most nuts can be bought either in the shell or shelled, and some are further processed by blanching, flaking or grinding (almonds, for instance). Some nuts such as chestnuts are cultivated for flour, and chestnuts were once a staple in northern Italy (the original polenta).

If using nuts in recipes it is my preference to buy them in the shell and then shell them at home. This is time-consuming perhaps, but worth it, as the flavour is very definitely superior. Good nuts taste sweet, have a crisp texture and a plump appearance. Stale nuts will taste rancid and unpleasant and look shrivelled.

Many types of nuts are cultivated as much for their oil as their kernels – amongst them walnuts, hazelnuts, peanuts and almonds. Many are also made into liqueurs in Italy, where, the further south you go, the more nuts appear in cooking as a protein alternative. We also use nuts in salads, sauces, biscuits, cakes, sweets and ice-cream.

INSALATA DI PECORINO E NOCI
cheese and walnut salad

This simple salad illustrates how something wonderful can be produced when you use a few ingredients at their peak of perfection – the fennel, walnuts and oil. A good, aged Pecorino is something worth seeking out from your local cheese shop – there really isn't a substitute.

SERVES 4

400g (14oz) mature Pecorino

2 Florence fennel bulbs, trimmed

a handful of fresh rocket leaves

12 whole walnuts, freshly shelled

3 tbsp Tuscan extra virgin olive oil

sea salt and freshly ground black pepper

1 Cut the cheese and fennel bulbs into thin slices.

2 Arrange the rocket leaves around the edge of the serving dish. Put the cheese and fennel in the centre and the walnuts on top. Sprinkle with oil, salt and pepper and serve.

PERE CON GORGONZOLA
pears with walnuts and gorgonzola

My friend Michaela introduced this idea to me while I was teaching in her home in Florence one autumn. The walnuts were fresh from the trees in the garden, as were the pears. Even the honey was home-produced, and everything tasted quite remarkable.

SERVES 4

45g (1½oz) walnuts, freshly shelled

4 pears, peeled, cored and cut into thin wedges

115g (4oz) sweet Gorgonzola

local fragrant honey for drizzling

1 Preheat the oven to 200°C / 400°F / gas mark 6.

2 Place the walnuts on a baking sheet and toast for six to seven minutes until golden.

3 Arrange the pear wedges on individual plates, crumble the Gorgonzola over the pears, and top with the toasted walnuts. Drizzle honey over each serving and serve immediately.

SUGO DI NOCI
walnut sauce

My sister has two magnificent walnut trees in her garden in England, and they produce a profusion of nuts. One day I found her on her hands and knees picking up nuts from the ground and wondering in despair what she could do with them. I remembered this recipe – it's a sort of winter pesto – from a recent trip, and we spent the afternoon shelling walnuts and making the sauce. We had enough to keep her going for quite a while – and to give as Christmas presents! The sauce is wonderful with potato gnocchi (see page 34).

SERVES 6

175g (6oz) shelled walnuts (for perfection, just out of the shell or vacuum-sealed which tend to be sweeter)

1 garlic clove

a handful of fresh basil leaves, roughly torn

55g (2oz) Pecorino Romano, freshly grated

55g (2oz) Parmesan, freshly grated

40g (1½oz) unsalted butter

4 tbsp extra virgin olive oil

sea salt and freshly ground black pepper

85ml (3fl oz) double cream

1 Place the walnuts and garlic in a food processor. Process until finely chopped.

2 Add the basil, cheeses, butter and oil and process just a little bit more.

3 Transfer the mixture to a bowl and season with salt and pepper. Mix in the cream.

4 Refrigerate until needed. It will last one week. Use pasta or gnocchi water to slacken the sauce prior to serving.

BISCOTTI
lemon walnut biscuits

Biscotti are great to have in a tin in the kitchen. They last a while, they are good for dunking into Vinsanto (the 'holy' wine of Tuscany), and are wonderful to give as a present, wrapped in cellophane. The hint of butter gives these particular biscotti great flavour.

48 BISCUITS

40g (1½oz) unsalted butter, plus extra for greasing

100g (3½oz) golden caster sugar

2 large eggs

1-2 tsp vanilla extract

finely grated zest and juice of 2 lemons

225g (8oz) Italian 00 plain flour

¼ tsp baking powder

100g (3½oz) walnuts, coarsely chopped

1 Preheat the oven to 200°C / 400°F / gas mark 6. Grease a 25 x 38cm (10x15in) baking sheet.

2 Beat together the measured butter, sugar and eggs, mixing well. Add the vanilla, lemon zest and juice.

3 Combine the flour, baking powder, and walnuts, and add to the egg mixture, mixing well.

4 The dough will be stiff and sticky but with floured hands, divide the dough in half on the baking sheet. Pat each half out into a loaf 30cm (12in) long and roughly 5cm (2in) wide. Space the loaves at least 7.5cm (3in) apart. Flatten slightly. Bake for 20 minutes in the preheated oven until firm and lightly brown.

5 Remove from the oven and place the baking sheet on a wire rack to cool slightly. Reduce the oven temperature to 150°C / 300°F / gas mark 2.

6 While they are still slightly warm, slice the loaves on the diagonal into 1cm (½in) slices. Arrange the slices, cut side down, on the baking sheet, return to the oven and bake for 15 minutes more or until dry. Place on a wire rack to cool completely.

TORTA DI CAROTE
carrot and almond cake

Carrots don't feature heavily in Italian cooking, but Italians are really fond of this cake the length and breadth of the country, probably because of the nut content. My friend Luisa from Barletta gave me this variation. I think I must have collected about a dozen recipes for carrot cake by now, but this one has been worth repeating again and again.

SERVES 8

unsalted butter for greasing

plain flour for dusting

250g (9oz) golden caster sugar

250g (9oz) ground almonds

250g (9oz) organic carrots, grated

1 tbsp Amaretto liqueur

5 large eggs, separated

½ tsp baking powder

2 tsp vanilla extract

vanilla icing sugar

1 Preheat the oven to 180°C / 350°F / gas mark 4, and butter and flour a 25cm (10in) round cake tin.

2 Mix the sugar, almonds, carrots, Amaretto, egg yolks, baking powder and vanilla extract together.

3 Whisk the egg whites until firm and fold them lightly into the carrot mixture.

4 Turn the mixture into the prepared tin. Bake for 45 minutes in the preheated oven until a skewer comes out clean.

5 Place on a wire rack to cool. Dust with vanilla icing sugar.

RICCIARELLI DI SIENA
almond biscuits from siena

It really is worth using a pestle and mortar to finely crush the nuts, as the essential oils are slowly released and therefore make for a more natural flavour. The resting of the mixture is important too, as it allows even more flavour to develop. I usually make these biscuits first thing in the morning and they are ready by lunchtime, to be enjoyed throughout the rest of the day, with an espresso. They're great as a gift too!

ABOUT 30 BISCUITS

225g (8oz) blanched almonds

55g (2oz) pine nuts

115g (4oz) granulated sugar

55g (2oz) icing sugar, plus extra for dusting

2 tsp grated unwaxed orange zest

3 large egg whites, beaten to stiff peaks

1 Using a pestle and mortar, finely crush the almonds and pine kernels.

2 Place this mixture in a large bowl, add the sugar, icing sugar and orange zest and stir until well blended. Gently fold the beaten egg whites into the nut mixture.

3 Shape the biscuits using 2 tsp and place on a baking tray lined with greaseproof paper. Rest for six hours.

4 Preheat the oven to 180°C / 350°F / gas mark 4. Bake the biscuits in the preheated oven for 15 minutes until golden.

5 Remove the biscuits from the oven and cool on a wire rack. Serve at room temperature dusted with icing sugar.

STRAZZATE
chocolate almond biscuits

This recipe comes from Basilicata, on the Adriatic coast of Italy. Little is known of the cuisine of this region, but they do love nuts. These biscuits are made from the classical recipe, but each home would have its own variation.

ABOUT 30 BISCUITS

1 Preheat the oven to 200°C / 400°F / gas mark 6.

2 Combine all of the ingredients except for the Strega in a bowl. Then add the liqueur and mix to a firm dough. Add more flour if necessary to make sure the dough is firm, or if it is *too* firm add some more water, a bit at a time.

3 In your fingers, pinch off little chunks of dough about the size of an almond. Pat these chunks down onto a surface to form 2.5cm (1in) squares, then place on a greased baking sheet.

4 Bake for 10–15 minutes until the biscuits are slightly chewy and springy, but not browned. Cool before serving.

200g (7oz) blanched and toasted almonds, coarsely chopped

200g (7oz) Italian 00 plain flour

100g (3½oz) caster sugar

55g (2oz) rich cocoa powder

55g (2oz) best-quality chocolate, shaved in strips

4 tbsp Strega liqueur

LENTICCHIE ALLA MONTANARA
lentils with chestnuts

Lentils are infinitely versatile, and very good for you. I think those from Castelluccio are the best, but I'm slightly biased, having spent a good deal of time in Umbria watching the back-breaking harvest of these 'freckles', as the Italians call them. When roasting chestnuts, slash with a sharp knife first to prevent them exploding in the oven. Roast for 25–35 minutes in an oven preheated to about 180°C / 350°F / gas mark 4. They are easier to skin whilst warm.

SERVES 8

2 tbsp olive oil

4 garlic cloves, peeled and crushed

400g (14oz) Castelluccio lentils

a handful of fresh thyme leaves, chopped

2 bay leaves

150g (5½oz) canned Italian plum tomatoes

25 chestnuts, roasted and roughly chopped

a pinch of dried chilli (peperoncino)

4 tbsp estate-bottled extra virgin olive oil

sea salt and freshly ground black pepper

a handful of fresh flat–leaf parsley leaves
to garnish

1 In a saucepan, heat the olive oil, then add the garlic and lentils. Stir to coat the lentils with the oil and garlic. Add the thyme and bay. Cover generously with cold water, place a lid on the pan and simmer gently for 20–30 minutes. Keep checking the pan; the water must not completely evaporate.

2 Add the tomatoes, chestnuts and peperoncino, and continue simmering for 20 minutes. Add salt and pepper to taste. Garnish with extra virgin olive oil and parsley leaves, and serve with Pizza Bianca (see p212).

BUDINO DI CASTAGNE
chestnut pudding

My father grows chestnuts and exports them to the French for marrons glacés. In his research he has found them to be totally organic, in that the trees do not need fertilising or any help at all from man. They look after themselves from start to finish. To check whether a chestnut is still fresh, place in a bowl of cold water. Unsound nuts will bob to the top, so they can be discarded.

SERVES 6

500g (1lb 2oz) fresh chestnuts

1 tsp vanilla extract

4 tbsp dark rum

100g (3½oz) golden granulated sugar

250ml (9fl oz) double cream

juice of 1 orange

1 Make a nick in the skin of each chestnut with a sharp knife. Boil the chestnuts in water to cover for 20–30 minutes. Peel off the outer skin, remove the inner skin, and press the flesh through a ricer or sieve while still hot.

2 Add the vanilla, rum and sugar. Mix well and chill.

3 Beat the cream until stiff, and gradually add the orange juice.

4 Add the puréed chestnuts to the cream and beat together thoroughly. Place in the fridge until well chilled.

5 Serve with a chocolate sauce or bitter chocolate ice cream.

ROCCIATE
fruit and nut biscuits

This represents total fruit and nut indulgence, a bringing together of autumn's finest fruits and nuts. The biscuits are totally healthy, and wonderful to have on a long car journey when you need a burst of energy. They would be good in a child's packed lunch too.

ABOUT 12 BISCUITS

115g (4oz) dried prunes

55g (2oz) raisins

55g (2oz) dried figs, stemmed and sliced

2 apples, peeled, cored and sliced

55g (2oz) shelled hazelnuts, coarsely chopped

55g (2oz) blanched almonds, coarsely chopped

55g (2oz) shelled walnuts, coarsely chopped

55g (2oz) pine kernels

50ml (2fl oz) Marsala

5 tbsp olive oil

150g (5½oz) caster sugar

200g (7oz) Italian 00 plain flour

a pinch of sea salt

icing sugar for dusting

1 Soak the dried prunes and raisins in lukewarm water for half an hour. Drain and pit the prunes.

2 Mix the fruit and nuts in a bowl. Add the Marsala, 1 tbsp of the oil and 85g (3oz) of the sugar.

3 Sift the flour and salt together, mix in the remaining oil and sugar and enough water to make a soft dough. Form it into a ball and let it rest, covered, for 30 minutes.

4 Preheat the oven to 180°C / 350°F / gas mark 4.

5 Divide the dough into 12 equal pieces. Roll out each piece into a very thin square. Spread some of the fruit mixture on each square of dough, dividing it evenly. Roll the squares up into cylinders and place on a lightly greased baking sheet.

5 Bake in the preheated oven until golden brown, about 30 minutes. Leave to cool.

6 Sprinkle with icing sugar and serve.

TORTA DI NOCCIOLE
hazelnut cake

Hazelnuts are probably the most favoured nuts in Italy. They are used in many biscuits and cakes, and Frangelico, a hazelnut liqueur (sold in a friar-shaped bottle!), is a great hit with all who try it. This cake is a classic from Piedmont, at the foot of the mountains. I like to think that hazelnuts create a source of energy for the farmers there during the autumn and winter, as they never seem to stop at that time of year: the vendemmia, the grape harvest, is immediately followed by the olive harvest...

SERVES 6

300g (10½oz) hazelnuts

200g (7oz) Italian 00 plain flour, plus extra for dusting

2 tsp baking powder

3 largest eggs

150g (5½oz) golden caster sugar

100g (3½oz) unsalted butter, melted and cooled to room temperature, plus extra for greasing

50ml (2fl oz) brewed Italian espresso coffee

50ml (2fl oz) whole milk

2 tbsp light rum

1 tbsp olive oil

1 tsp vanilla extract

8 amaretti cookies, crushed

1 Preheat the oven to 190°C / 375°F / gas mark 5. Butter a 23cm (9in) cake tin and lightly dust with flour.

2 Spread the hazelnuts on a baking sheet and toast them in the preheated oven for 10 minutes until golden brown. Cool completely. When cool, finely grind them in a food processor.

3 Sift the measured flour and the baking powder together.

4 Beat the eggs and sugar in a large bowl for one minute using an electric mixer on high speed. Switch the speed to low and blend in the melted, measured butter, the coffee, milk, rum, olive oil and vanilla. When well blended, stir in the ground nuts and amaretti biscuits.

5 Add the flour to the mixture and beat gently. Pour the mixture into the prepared cake tin.

6 Bake in the centre of the preheated oven for 40–45 minutes. Cool for 10 minutes then turn out onto a cooling rack. Cool completely before serving.

INVERNO

winter

'It's good food and not fine words that keeps me alive.'

Molière (1622–1673)

CAVOLO NERO CON LE FETTE

toasted bread with tuscan black cabbage and cannellini beans

I'm a great advocate of cooking your own pulses. It makes an enormous amount of difference to the overall flavour. I served this dish recently to my students, and sensed a lack of enthusiasm. The more I praised the dish, the more I felt my confidence slipping away. Eventually, when the dish was ready and drizzled with really good olive oil, I got some approving looks and my faith in my taste-buds was restored. This is the sort of food I love best – it's not at all elegant, just good and honest.

SERVES 6

450g (1lb) cavolo nero

200g (7oz) cooked dried white cannellini beans

6 slightly dry slices firm-textured, country-style bread

1 large garlic clove, peeled

extra virgin olive oil for drizzling

sea salt and freshly ground black pepper

CAVOLO NERO

black cabbage – available only in the winter in Italy – is a member of the Brassica family. It is a tall, elegant vegetable, and its very dark green leaves herald the onset of winter. If I ever get married, I'd like to use cavolo nero as part of my bouquet – I think the colour is beautiful, particularly against bridal white! Cavolo nero is grown mainly in central Italy, and is a fundamental ingredient in the famous soup, la ribollita; it is also eaten with beans on bruschetta, or briefly stewed and served warm with hot oil, garlic and lemon juice. Look out for this delicious green – I have seen it in supermarkets.

1 Cut the cavolo nero into 5cm (2in) pieces.

2 Fill a pan with 1 litre (1¾ pints) water. Bring to the boil, add some salt and the carolo nero, and simmer for 10–15 minutes until tender.

3 Warm up the beans in a little water in a small saucepan. Preheat the oven to 200°C / 400°F / gas mark 6.

4 Arrange the bread slices in a single layer on a baking sheet and bake them for three minutes. Turn over and bake for three minutes more. While the bread is hot, rub one side with the garlic clove.

5 Arrange the bread on plates, garlic side up. Scoop the cavolo nero from the pot using a skimmer or slotted spoon, and arrange on the bread slices. Spoon the drained hot beans over the cavolo nero. Drizzle with olive oil, season with salt and pepper, and serve immediately.

LA RIBOLLITA
're-boiled soup'

Tuscans cook la ribollita with black cabbage, which comes into season just as the new olive oil is pressed in November. The oil is an important element and should not be overlooked. Make as much of this soup as fits comfortably in your largest casserole – the quantities below are simply a basic guide. Like many other soups, it improves if left for a day. The texture should be wet, but not a broth.

SERVES 8

175g (6oz) dried cannellini beans

1 large onion, sliced

4 carrots, chopped

4 celery sticks, trimmed and chopped

4 leeks, washed, trimmed and chopped

250g (9oz) cavolo nero, trimmed and washed

8 tomatoes

4 tbsp olive oil

2 cloves of garlic, minced

1 dried chilli (peperoncino), crumbled, seeds and all

a handful of fresh herbs (parsley, bay and rosemary), chopped

sea salt and freshly ground black pepper

2 tbsp olive oil

To serve:

8 slices country-style bread

new season extra virgin olive oil (estate-bottled)

3 tbsp chopped fresh flat-leaf parsley

1 Soak the cannellini beans overnight in cold water. Drain and rinse.

2 Thinly slice the onion. Chop the carrots, celery, leeks and carolo nero. Blanch the tomatoes in boiling water, drain, skin, quarter and seed.

3 Sweat the onion in a large flameproof casserole in half of the oil. Add the rest of the vegetables and the tomatoes and mix so they are liberally covered in oil. Add half the garlic and the chilli pepper. Cook for 10 minutes.

4 Add the beans and stir. Cover with water, then simmer slowly covered, for one and a half to two hours, or until the beans are soft.

5 Remove a third of the soup mixture and mash or liquidise to a purée. Return to the casserole.

6 In a separate pan, warm the remaining oil, and sauté the remaining minced garlic, along with the herbs, and brown lightly. Add to the casserole. Leave for 24 hours.

7 Warm through uncovered. The mixture must be wet but not sloppy. Season to taste. Lay a slice of bread on the bottom of a soup bowl, ladle the ribollita over and then pour over a generous – don't stint – amount of extra virgin olive oil, with a sprinkling of salt and parsley.

ZUPPA ALLA FRANTOIANA
olive press soup

This is the perfect soup-meal, as it contains so many great vegetables. It's light, though, despite the bean content, improves with keeping, and is a real winter warmer. Do investigate a good supplier of borlotti beans; these are more floury than cannellini, which means they soak up more flavour. This recipe is typical of Tuscany, where they make such a fuss about their new oil.

SERVES 8

2 tbsp olive oil

2 medium carrots, trimmed and finely chopped

1 celery stick, trimmed and finely choppes

1 medium red onion, peeled and finely chopped

2 leeks, trimmed and finely chopped

2 garlic cloves, peeled

a handful of fresh sage leaves, torn

1 medium head Savoy cabbage, shredded

5 cavolo nero leaves and stalks, roughly chopped

1x400 g (14oz) can Italian plum tomatoes

6 new potatoes, peeled and diced

3 small courgettes, trimmed and sliced

1 medium Florence fennel bulb, roughly chopped

a handful of fresh basil leaves

1 tsp fresh thyme leaves

a pinch of freshly grated nutmeg

500g (1lb 2oz) cooked borlotti beans, cooked with garlic and sage (retain the cooking water)

sea salt and freshly ground pepper

4 tbsp or more new season extra virgin olive oil (estate bottled)

1 Heat the olive oil in a large soup pan over a low heat. Add the carrot, celery, onions, leeks, garlic and sage and cook for about 10 minutes, stirring frequently, until translucent.

2 Add the cabbage, carolo nero and tomatoes and their juices, and stir well until blended. Cook for 10 minutes.

3 Add 1 litre (1¾ pints) water along with the remaining vegetables, herbs and spices, increase the heat to medium and cook for 45 minutes.

4 Pass the beans and their liquid through a food mill and add the mass to the soup pan. Heat well again and adjust the seasoning. Divide the soup between bowls and anoint with the new season's oil. You may like to serve this with Parmesan.

RAVIOLI CON CICORIA
green chicory ravioli

We Italians just love our greens. As a filling for ravioli, the slightly bitter cicoria leaves provide a perfect foil for the sweeter tomato sauce, but you could use spinach, Swiss chard or rocket instead. I first enjoyed this dish in Venice in a little café on a very cold day in February before the Carnival. It was cooked by the grandmother of the family. I went back for dinner and had the same dish again, just so that I could commit the flavour to memory...

SERVES 4

Pasta:

2 eggs (the largest you can find)

115g (4oz) Italian 00 plain flour

115g (4oz) semolina flour

sea salt

Filling:

500g (1lb 2oz) chicory leaves, trimmed

sea salt and freshly ground black pepper

250g (9oz) ricotta cheese, fresh if possible (or tub ricotta)

1 garlic clove, peeled and crushed

a pinch of peperoncino dried chilli to taste

1 egg (the largest again)

100g (3½oz) Parmesan, freshly grated

To serve:

55g (2oz) unsalted butter

freshly grated Parmesan cheese

Tomato sauce (see page 147)

1 Make the pasta as described on page 151. Roll as described, then cut into 7.5cm (3in) wide strips.

2 To start the stuffing, boil the trimmed leaves in boiling salted water for seven to 10 minutes until tender, then drain well and finely chop.

3 Mix together the ricotta, garlic, chilli, egg, Parmesan cheese, salt and pepper to taste. Make little balls and put them on a pasta strip, about 7.5cm (2½in) apart. Cover with another pasta strip, seal and cut apart with a ravioli cutter. Continue until all the dough and filling are used up. Dry for a while.

4 Simmer the ravioli in salted water for about eight minutes, or until they bob to the top of the water. Drain and serve with the butter, Parmesan and warmed tomato sauce.

CICORIA
chicory/endive

The variety of chicories we are familiar with today all descend from a wild chicory native to Europe, western Asia and Africa. The leaves are small, toothed like dandelion, and taste very bitter. Over the centuries, the plant was cultivated, and larger leaved and less bitter varieties were developed. Cultivated chicories appear in two basic types, both of which are Cichorium. C. intybus includes: green leafy plants, most of which are more familiar in Italy, amongst them catalogna; red-leaved types, amongst them radicchio di Treviso (long) and radicchio di Chioggia (round); and the white compact torpedo which we know in Britain as chicory or Belgian endive. The latter was developed in France and Belgium in the late nineteenth century. Close relatives with large roots were the source of a substitute coffee common in Europe from the middle of the eighteenth century (when imported real coffee was very expensive). C. endivia is the plant we know in Britain as endive, and other cultivars are known variously as frisée, batavia and escarole. Most members of the chicory family are eaten raw in salads, although they can be cooked as well. Green cicoria leaves are delicious in a ravioli stuffing mixed with ricotta cheese. My grandmother used to sauté leaves with olive oil and garlic, one of my earliest taste memories. Italians love to include any of the chicories regularly in their diet as a liver cleanser. They are obsessed with keeping the liver in good condition...

FARRO CON FAGIOLI
farro and bean soup

Barley-like and light brown, farro has recently been rediscovered and is now valued both for its taste and nutritional value. Farro is cultivated almost exclusively in the Garfagnana, the mountainous region of Tuscany, and its use has brought a fresh recognition to Tuscan cooking. This soup is typical of the Garfagnana.

SERVES 8

250g (9oz) dried borlotti beans, soaked overnight, drained and rinsed

2 medium white onions, peeled

5 sage leaves

3 garlic cloves, peeled

4 tbsp olive oil

1 medium red onion, peeled and finely chopped

2 carrots, scraped and diced

2–4 celery sticks, trimmed and diced

a handful of flat-leaf parsley leaves

275g (9½oz) canned Italian plum tomatoes and their liquid

6 tbsp extra virgin olive oil (estate bottled)

200g (7oz) farro, soaked overnight, drained and rinsed

sea salt and freshly ground black pepper

1 Place the beans in a large saucepan with one onion, half the sage, one of the garlic cloves, and enough water to cover by at least 5cm (2in).

2 Cover and cook for one hour or until tender. When the beans are cooked, pass the contents of the pan either through a food processor or a mouli di légumes.

3 Heat the oil in a large saucepan. Add the red onion and the remaining white onion, which have been finely chopped. Add the carrots, celery, most of the parsley, remaining garlic and sage leaves, the tomatoes and 3 tbsp of hot water; continue to cook for 10 minutes.

4 Add the farro and simmer on a low heat for 30 minutes until tender. Add salt and pepper and the bean mixture. Stir and warm through until hot. Adjust the seasoning and serve with drizzlings of olive oil and the remaining parsley.

FARRO

farro is a grain which is related to wheat, actually a type of spelt, which was cultivated and eaten by the Assyrians, Egyptians and Romans. The latter boiled the kernels in a stew, and used the flour in a type of polenta. Farro is planted in autumn on graduated terraces rather like rice. However it does not like 'standing' in water like rice, which is why it does so well in mountainous country. The grain is resistant to disease and

therefore needs no fungicides or pesticides, so it is totally organic. It is harvested in June: the stalks are cut from the fields and allowed to dry for a few months before being beaten to remove the kernels. There are two types of farro: the grain farro and Triticum spelta, also called farricello or spelt. The difference between the two types is that farro needs a 12-hour soaking period, while spelt can be cooked without soaking.

ALLORO

bay

The bay tree, Laurus nobilis, originated in Asia Minor and the Mediterranean. It belongs to the Lauraceae family, along with – perhaps surprisingly – cassia, cinnamon, sassafras and the avocado. It has long been used in European, particularly Mediterranean, cooking, and has a major place in history and legend. One of the most romantic myths of antiquity tells of Apollo's love for Daphne, daughter of the river god. Struck by Cupid's arrow, Apollo pursued Daphne, but she loved only hunting and solitude. One day he gave chase, and as she ran to escape him she prayed for the earth to enclose and save her. As Apollo gained on her, her legs became roots and her arms and hair branches. And when Apollo finally embraced her, he held in his arms only the trunk of a tree, the bay laurel. From then on, Apollo chose the bay as his emblem and crowned himself with its leaves – the origin of the crown of laurel given to honour achievements in music, letters, science, sports and battle, and of the title 'laureate'.

The bay is an evergreen shrub or tree that can grow to 6m (20ft) in height. The bark is greenish, but it becomes dark as the tree matures. The leaves are oblong, tough and shiny on top, from 5–10cm (2–4in) in length, sometimes with wavy edges. The tree flowers in April. The fruit, often called a berry, is actually a drupe which, like an olive or peach, consists of fruit flesh containing one seed. These little buds can be seen on bay branches at most times of the year. They should be harvested when ripe, and dried in a bread oven after making bread, or in a very low oven overnight. Both leaves and drupes, fresh and dried, are highly and pleasantly scented.

All over Europe, bay leaves are used in a bouquet garni or aromi, and in savoury soups, stews and marinades. In Britain they are often used for flavouring custards and milk puddings. Try to use fresh leaves if you can as they are stronger; the drier the leaf becomes, the more it loses the essential oil that is the source of the flavour and aroma.

BACLAURO
bay liqueur

This bay liqueur, based on dried bay drupes, is made almost everywhere in Sicily and anywhere the bay tree grows. And as bay trees grow so readily in Britain, I couldn't resist including the recipe. I think it has a curious taste, but it is perfect after dinner. If you cannot find pure alcohol (difficult in Britain), use a good vodka.

450g (1lb) dried bay drupes

2 tsp vanilla extract

1.5 litres (2¾ pints) pure 95% alcohol (or vodka)

2kg (4½lb) granulated sugar

2.8 litres (5 pints) pure distilled water

1 Marinate the dried drupes with the vanilla and alcohol for 15 days.

2 Then make a sugar syrup with the sugar and pure water: simmer gently until the sugar has dissolved, then leave to cool.

3 Add the syrup to the alcohol mixture and filter the concoction through muslin into sterilised bottles. Keep for two months in a dark place before using.

PANE ALL'ANICE E ALLORO
anise and bay crown loaf

This recipe evolved out of sheer necessity, and my love of aniseeds and bay leaves. I thought the two would marry well, and indeed they do. The bread looks wonderful as well! It is good served with very savoury foods, but is equally delicious toasted for breakfast. I've offered it with cheese at the end of a meal, and that's been popular too.

SERVES 10

Bread dough:

1 tsp anise seeds

250ml (9fl oz) spring water

1 tbsp clear honey

250ml (9fl oz) whole milk

1 tsp fresh yeast

500–550g (18–20oz) strong white flour, preferably organic

3 tsp sea salt

2 tbsp olive oil

10 bay leaves

Egg wash:

1 large egg yolk

1 tsp water

1 To make the bread dough: put the aniseeds and water in a small saucepan and boil for five minutes. Pour the mixture into a large bowl, then stir in the honey and milk. Let the mixture cool to 40–46°C / 104–115°F.

2 Sprinkle the yeast over the warm liquid and stir until the yeast has completely dissolved. Add the flour 115g (4oz) at a time, then add the salt. Use only enough flour to make a soft dough. Turn the dough out on to a lightly floured board and knead for 10 minutes incorporating more flour if necessary to keep the dough from sticking to the board. The dough should be smooth and tender.

3 Transfer the ball of dough to a large bowl and drizzle the olive oil over it. Cover with a kitchen towel and leave to rise for an hour, or until doubled in size.

4 Preheat the oven to 200°C / 400°F / gas mark 6. Oil a large baking sheet.

5 When the dough is ready, turn it out on to a board and knead for two minutes to knock out the gases. Flour the dough lightly, wrap it in the towel and let it rest for five minutes.

6 Roll the dough into a 28cm (11in) long rope. Twist the rope several times and arrange it on the baking sheet in a ring. Pinch the ends together and tuck them under. Make 10 diagonal slashes on the surface and tuck a bay leaf into each slash. Cover the dough and let it rest for 25–30 minutes.

7 Make the egg wash by beating the egg yolk and water together in a small bowl. Brush the egg wash over the surface of the dough.

8 Bake the bread for 30–35 minutes in the preheated oven until golden, and the base sounds hollow when knocked. Cool on a wire rack.

PREZZEMOLO

parsley originated in the Mediterranean. There are two major forms of parsley, but flat-leaf parsley – also called Italian parsley – is the species mainly cultivated today in Italy. We believe the flavour is more pungent than that of curly parsley, the type commonly seen and used in Britain. Parsley seeds are tiny and black, and were once used in cooking. They germinate slowly, taking up to 90 days to sprout. The intensity of the aroma of fresh parsley depends on the climate in which it is grown, and nothing can beat flat-leaf parsley, which has developed in the heat of southern Italy. I use the herb liberally in most of my dishes. To me, it's like salt, vital for flavour. It can be used in soups, pesto, in a salsa verde and in many other sauces.

ZUPPA DI PREZZEMOLO
parsley soup

Parsley is the garnish for this soup, but it's no ordinary garnish. It represents a real mouthful of flavours, very similar to the classical gremolata that dresses osso buco.

SERVES 6

2 large old potatoes, peeled and cubed

1 carrot, peeled and cubed

2 celery sticks, trimmee and diced

1 onion, peeled and roughly diced

500g (18oz) young spinach leaves

sea salt and freshly ground black pepper

Parsley topping:

a handful of flat-leaf parsley leaves, chopped

rind of 1 unwaxed lemon, finely chopped

2 garlic cloves, peeled and crushed

4 tbsp excellent fruity oil

150g (5½oz) Parmesan cheese, grated

1 Put the potatos, carrot, celery, onion, spinach and some salt in a pan. Cover with water and cook until the potatoes start to break up, at least 30 minutes.

2 Meanwhile, mix all the topping ingredients together, seasoning with salt and peppers, and set aside.

3 Remove the soup from the heat. Check the seasoning. Pour the soup into a tureen and sprinkle the parsley mixture on top.

FUME DI PESCE
fish broth

This is a very important basic broth used in my family (it's another of my grandmother's recipes) for soups, fish casseroles, fish risottos and sauces. A fish broth was made weekly, revealing the Italian tendency to frugality, never allowing even fish bones to go to waste – although some of them did go to the cat!

MAKES ABOUT 450ML (¾ PINT)

25g (1oz) unsalted butter

55g (2oz) onions, peeled and chopped

675g–900g (1½–2lb) white fish bones, cleaned

2 sprigs fresh thyme

2 bay leaves

1 chopped stick of celery

a handful of fresh flat-leafed parsley leaves and stalks

1 tsp white peppercorns

1 Melt the butter in a large saucepan, add the onion and let it sweat for five minutes.

2 Add the fish bones and thyme, bay leaves, celery, parsley and peppercorns. Cook for five minutes stirring constantly.

3 Add 1 litre (1¾ pints) water, bring to the boil, then reduce to a simmer for 20 minutes, uncovered.

4 Strain the stock through a conical sieve, cool and refrigerate.

CARDI FRITTI AL POMODORO
fried cardoon with tomato sauce

It delights me to see the ever-increasing range of vegetables now available in supermarkets and good grocers. Cardoons may be rare as yet in Britain, but will surely soon appear on the list. This method of cooking vegetables – dusting in flour, coating with egg and then deep-frying – can be applied to aubergines, courgettes and fennel.

SERVES 6

1.5kg (3lb 5oz) cardoons

juice of 1 lemon

4 tbsp olive oil

3 garlic cloves, peeled and crushed

500g (1lb 2oz) ripe tomatoes, chopped

sea salt and freshly ground black pepper

olive oil for deep-frying

125g (4oz) Italian 00 plain flour

2 large eggs, beaten with a pinch of salt

a handful of fresh flat-leaf parsley leaves, finely chopped

CARDO

wild cardoons which grow all over the Mediterranean, are thistles, and are probably the ancestors of the globe artichoke and the cultivated cardoon. The wild plants are so thorny that you can hardly walk in the fields where they grow. Before the globe artichoke developed, the Ancient Romans and Greeks regarded the cardoon as a delicacy, and it is still only in Europe that the plant is truly appreciated. Cardoons grow like a big head of celery, with a profusion of leaves, but it is the stalks that are eaten rather than the leaves or the flower heads. The flavour of the stalks is not unlike the globe artichoke, but the texture is more celery-like. The raw stalks are a vital ingredient in the anchovy dip bagna cauda. The stalks are also parboiled and served baked in a cheese sauce.

1 Clean the cardoons, removing the leaves and peeling the outer strings. The central part *cuore di cardi*, the heart – is the best. Cut into small pieces and as each is prepared, drop it into a bowl of water acidulated with the lemon juice. Do not soak for longer than five minutes.

2 Heat the olive oil in a saucepan over a medium heat. Add the garlic and tomatoes and season with salt and pepper. Cook, covered, over a low heat until the sauce is dense, about 20 minutes.

3 Bring plenty of salted water to the boil in a large saucepan. Drop in the cardoons and cook until tender but still firm, about eight minutes. Drain, rinse under cold running water and dry on kitchen paper.

4 Heat the oil. Dredge the cardoons in the flour and dip in the egg. Deep-fry until crisp and golden on all sides. Drain the cardoons on paper towels, transfer to a serving plate and keep warm.

5 Stir the parsley into the hot tomato sauce and serve the fried cardoons and sauce together.

ANGUILLA ALL'UVETTA
eel   with   raisins

Please do not be afraid of eels. They may look unprepossessingly snake-like, but the flavour and texture are outstanding. Eels are loved in London – the famous jellied eels particularly – but somehow they still have a bad image. This recipe should convert you, as it is blissfully straightforward. Get your fishmonger to skin the fish for you.

SERVES 6

4 tbsp olive oil

200g (7oz) fresh porcini or field mushrooms, cleaned and sliced

sea salt and freshly ground black pepper

juice of ½ lemon

2 tbsp raisins

1kg (2¼lb) eel, skinned

15g (½oz) unsalted butter

1 onion, peeled and sliced

1 carrot, sliced

2 garlic cloves, peels and crushed

1 tbsp Italian 00 plain flour

250ml (9fl oz) red wine

1 tbsp brandy

1 clove

2 bay leaves

7 fresh parsley sprigs

1 fresh rosemary sprig

175ml (6fl oz) water

1 Heat 2 tbsp of the olive oil in a frying pan over a moderate heat. Add the mushrooms and sauté for five minutes. Add some salt and pepper and squeeze lemon juice over the mushrooms. Cover the raisins with lukewarm water and let soak until needed.

2 Cut the eel into chunks, then wash and dry them. Heat the remaining oil with the butter in a frying pan. Add the onion and carrot and sauté over a moderate heat until the onion is translucent.

3 Add the pieces of eel and brown over a high heat for 10 minutes. Remove the eel and keep to one side. Add the garlic to the pan, and stir until fragrant. Stir in the flour then add the wine, brandy, clove, herbs and water. Cover and cook over a low heat for one hour, stirring occasionally.

4 Strain the sauce and transfer to a saucepan. Add the mushrooms, drained raisins and eel. Simmer to blend the flavours – about 25 minutes – then serve at once.

ANGUILLA

e e l s have an extraordinary life-cycle, living part of their lives in salt water, part in fresh. Mature eels are delicious, as are elvers (eel fry), both of which are highly valued in Italy. Eel is meaty, rich and satisfying, and in Italy is grilled, skewered, sautéed, stewed and preserved. Both the sea-dwelling conger and the fresh-water eel are smoked. The latter is pricier, but as it is so richly flavoured that you need little. If it has been hot-smoked, it needs no more cooking, and is best with lemon and bread. It is sold in long, thin, pale fawn fillets with a brownish-red strip.

The label in the image reads: M.P. VENERE L. 5000 and M.P. VENERE L. 4000

BACCALA'

salt cod with tomatoes and basil

Salt cod is a poverty food, born of the necessity to preserve gluts and to have food that would be edible in winter. I think it is quite a delicacy though, and with a tomato sauce it's great for children. My sister gives it to her family every Friday, and her five children all love it.

SERVES 6

675g (1½lb) dried salt cod, soaked in frequent changes of cold water for 24 hours

olive oil for frying

Italian 00 plain flour for dredging

3 garlic cloves peeled and chopped

700g (1lb 9oz) canned Italian plum tomatoes

1 medium dried chilli pepper (peperoncino), crumbled

sea salt and freshly ground black pepper

a handful of fresh basil leaves

BACCALA'

baccala is dried salt cod. First the fish is gutted and cleaned, then it is dry salted (usually on board), and dried. It seems to be particularly appreciated Mediterranean countries. It has been a popular food in these countries and elsewhere since early medieval times. It is tough-looking, hard and stiff (but not so stiff as stockfish, which is air-cured, unsalted cod). Salt cod is rather expensive, so if possible buy prime pieces from the middle, rather than from the tail and fin ends. The fish is creamy grey with a fine dusting of sparkling salt. It needs to be soaked for some 24 hours, with the water being changed frequently, until softened. In Italy it is sold ready to cook, and there are many regional recipes, a majority from the Veneto.

1 Dry the cod with paper towel and cut into pieces roughly 6cm (3¼ x 2½in). Heat 1cm (½in) olive oil in a large skillet over a medium heat. When hot, dredge the fish one piece at a time in the flour. Add several pieces to the hot oil and fry until golden and crisp on each side. Remove from the oil with a slotted spoon and drain on paper towels. Continue in this way until all the fish is fried.

2 Preheat the oven to 200°C / 400°F / gas mark 6.

3 Heat 2 tbsp of the olive oil in a large sauté pan. Add the garlic and cook until golden. Stir in the tomatoes, chilli pepper and some salt and pepper. Simmer for 15 minutes, breaking up the tomatoes with the back of a wooden spoon. If the sauce becomes too thick, add a little water to slacken it.

4 Arrange the fried salt cod in a single layer in a 33 x 23cm (13 x 9in) baking dish. Pour the sauce over the fish and bake in the preheated oven for 20 minutes. Serve immediately garnished with basil.

FONDUTA PIEMONTESE
fondue from piedmont

Here follows a classic recipe. Do be patient and plan ahead, it's well worth it, as I think this is food truly for the gods. I like to serve fonduta with fresh bread, toasted bread or grilled polenta. You ladle the cheese sauce over them.

SERVES 4

400g (14oz) Italian Fontina

300ml (½ pint), plus 2 tbsp full cream milk

55g (2oz) unsalted butter
(Italian if possible)

4 large egg yolks

sea salt and coarse ground black pepper

1 white truffle or 1 tbsp white truffle oil

1 About six hours before you want to serve the fonduta, cut the Fontina into small dice. Put in a medium-sized bowl and add enough milk just to cover the cheese. Set to one side.

2 Put the butter in a heatproof bowl over a pan of simmering water. Add the Fontina and milk and cook, stirring constantly until the cheese has melted; this should take about 10 minutes.

3 Beat in the egg yolks one at a time and continue cooking, beating the whole time until the egg has been absorbed and the sauce has the consistency of thick cream. Season with salt and pepper, transfer the fonduta to individual bowls. Slice the truffle on top, or drizzle with oil.

FONTINA

fontina is one of Italy's most delectable cheeses. It comes from the high Alpine meadows of the Valle d'Aosta, and is made with unpasteurised cows' milk in mountain chalets during the summer months. In winter the cheese is factory-made in the valleys. Fontina is deep golden yellow with a tough, almond-brown rind, a firm, slightly springy texture, and tiny holes. The flavour is nuttily delicate with subtle hints of honey, fruit and nuts, even of hay and wild mushrooms. It makes a memorable dessert cheese and is also an essential ingredient of fonduta, one of the great sauces of Piedmont.

PANE

bread is tasty all year round, but is particularly satisfying in the winter. It is a fundamental of the Italian table: it is eaten at most meals, and is vital for mopping up the delicious juices on the plate. We call this mopping-up process *un piccolo scarpe* ('the little shoe'). In Italy, bread is bought daily, sometimes twice daily, as it stales quickly. But nothing is wasted, as you will see in many recipes throughout this book.

Many of the breads of Italy are exciting in flavour and texture, but you can only find these in the countryside, in the villages, at traditional bakeries. In cities, breads are more humdrum, made for the masses. While taking the photographs for this book Jason, the photographer, Geoff, the designer, and I worked a night shift in a village bakery in order to get some interesting shots (see page 210). To me it was magic seeing how old traditions were still being adhered to.

Good breads use a *biga*, a dough starter, which I call 'my friend in the kitchen'. It is made daily in bakeries, and its acidic nature contributes to the flavour of the bread, to its chewy texture, and also makes the bread keep for slightly longer. Biga is quick to make, lasts for up to 72 hours, and transforms every bread made with it. I do urge you to bake some bread!

CIABATTA
'slipper' bread

These breads are eye-catching because of their dusty crusts and unusual shape, but they are more memorable for their extraordinary open texture and moist and chewy crumb. The Italian dialect word ciabatta translates as 'slipper', which gives some idea of its shape, something both flat and slightly puffy at the same time. To make successful ciabatta, you must have a dough which is so wet that it is almost unmanageable. But persevere!

The biga starter used here is different from the others following because it relies on a larger volume of flour to make flavour. You will have some biga left over, but hopefully this can be passed on to an equally enthusiastic friend to be used.

4 LOAVES

Biga starter (makes about 1 kg (2¼lb)):

5g (⅛oz) fresh yeast (or ½ teaspoon dried, but fresh is best)

400ml (14fl oz) water

550–600g (1¼lb – 1lb 5oz) strong white bread flour

Dough:

10g (¼oz) fresh yeast (or 1 teaspoon dried yeast, but fresh is best)

500g (1lb 2oz) *Biga* Starter (see above)

15g (½oz) fine sea salt

approx. 300ml (½ pint) warm water

To finish:

2–3 tbsp olive oil

500g (1lb 2oz) strong white bread flour

1 Mix the biga ingredients together and beat with a spoon or your hand until a loose dough has formed with no dry flour lumps. You should feel an elastic feeling as the gluten forms. Cover carefully and leave to sit at room temperature for 12–24 hours. You will use half of it for the ciabatta.

2 For the dough, mix everything together, keeping the olive oil back until the dough is roughly formed and some gluten is beginning to develop. It should be such a wet and sticky dough that it continually adheres to your hand in large elastic lumps. For this reason, many people prefer to make the dough in a mixer or food processor. Persevere with your chosen method of kneading until the gluten is well formed and you have achieved that elasticity and springiness that marks a good dough

3 Grease a large mixing bowl, bottom and sides, with liberal amounts of olive oil before dropping the dough into it and covering it carefully. The proving dough will be bathed in olive oil. During this rise, the dough will double or even triple its volume, taking one and a half to two hours to get there, perhaps even longer.

4 Gently ease the oily mass on to a well-floured work surface, trying as much as possible not to knock it down, thus keeping its puffiness and gas. With floured hands and tools, divide it into four pieces.

5 Grease two baking trays with olive oil. Gently roll each piece of dough in the flour lying on the surface and give it a hearty stretch as you pick it up to place it on the greased baking trays. (If you are going to bake it on a tile, place the stretched pieces on floured boards.) With the stretch you render each piece two or three times as long as it is wide. To push them out flat, you give them a few stabs with your fingertips but do not be too vigorous or they will be knocked down and toughened.

6 Cover the loaves loosely with cloths and clingfilm. Their final proving will take another hour. By the time they are ready to bake they will have risen, but not quite doubled in height. Although they still look oddly flat, don't worry, they will spring up in the oven.

7 Meanwhile, preheat the oven to 200°C / 400°F / gas mark 6.

8 Bake the loaves in the preheated oven, for barely 20 minutes.

PANE TOSCANO
tuscan bread

This is the recipe I elicited from the Tuscan baker where we laboured overnight – but considerably scaled down! There is a superstition in Italy that a loaf should always be served right side up, and that it is both unlucky and disrespectful to serve it upside down. My grandfather always made the sign of the Cross on fresh bread with a knife, signifying the importance of bread to him, the staff of life.

1 LARGE LOAF

Biga starter:

20g (¾oz) fresh yeast

250ml (9fl oz) warm water (pure)

200g (7oz) strong white bread flour or Italian 00 flour

Dough:

approx 250ml (9fl oz) warm water (pure)

fine sea salt

500g (1lb 2oz) strong white bread flour or Italian 00 flour

To finish:

olive oil

strong white bread flour

1 To make the biga starter: pour the warm water into a large glass bowl, sprinkle over the yeast and stir until dissolved. Add the flour and blend until the mixture is smooth. Sprinkle over a little extra bread flour and cover with a cloth for 24 hours.

2 To make the dough: stir the warm water and a large pinch of salt into the starter. Add 125g (4½oz) of flour at a time, blending thoroughly before adding the rest. Sprinkle 125g (4½oz) extra flour on to the work surface. Turn the dough onto the work surface and knead in all of the flour; this will take approximately 10 minutes. The dough will be sticky and difficult to handle at first, but after all the flour has been incorporated it should be easier to work with and tender.

3 Transfer the dough to a large oiled bowl. Rub the dough against the bowl to coat in oil. Cover with a damp cloth, and leave to rise for 45–60 minutes in a warm, draught-free place.

4 Punch down the dough to allow the gases to escape, and turn it onto a lightly floured board. Knead for five minutes. Shape the dough into a flat, wide loaf about 35cm (14in) long. Loosely wrap the dough in a towel, leaving enough room in the towel for the dough to rise. Let the dough rest again for 30–45 minutes; it will double in size.

5 Meanwhile, arrange terracotta tiles or a pizza stone on the centre shelf of the oven. Preheat the oven to 200°C / 400°F / gas mark 6 allowing 30 minutes for the oven to preheat.

6 When the dough is ready, roll it out of the towel directly on to the hot tiles or stone. Make one or more lengthwise slashes on the top of the bread using a sharp knife. Bake for 45–50 minutes in the preheated oven until lightly browned with a thick, hard crust. Turn the bread on its side and knock on the bottom. If done, you'll hear a hollow sound. Cool.

PIZZA BIANCA
white pizza

A typical Roman pizza would have many classic toppings, but this is the poor man's version, relying solely on the flavours of good oil, salt and rosemary. I often serve this when I'm cooking lunch for a large party of my pupils, as it's light, goes so well with so many dishes, and is easy on the digestion. The biga contributes to and enhances the flavour of the dough, and therefore makes it different from the classic pizza.

SERVES 4

Biga starter:

2.5g (¹⁄₁₆oz) fresh yeast

150ml (¼ pint) warm water (blood temperature)

125g (4½oz) strong white bread flour

Dough:

10g (¼oz) fresh yeast

175ml (6fl oz) warm water (blood temperature)

1½ tsp salt

375g (13oz) strong white bread flour

3 tbsp olive oil, plus extra for greasing

To finish:

olive oil

sea salt

fresh rosemary leaves

1 To make the biga starter: dissolve the fresh yeast in the warm water. Add the flour and mix to a smooth, thick batter. Cover and leave to ferment at room temperature for 12–36 hours until loose and bubbling.

2 To make the dough, dissolve the fresh yeast in half the warm water.

3 In a large bowl, mix the salt into the flour. Make a well in the centre, then pour in the yeast mixture, olive oil and biga, and combine. Add the remaining water, and mix to form a soft, sticky dough, adding extra water if necessary.

4 Turn the dough out onto a floured surface and knead until smooth, silky and elastic, about 10 minutes

5 Place the dough in a clean oiled bowl, cover and leave to rise until doubled in size, about one and a half to two hours.

6 Knock back and chafe (a rotating, shaping motion), then rest for 10 minutes.

7 Roll the dough out to a thickness of about 3mm (⅛in). Place on an oiled baking sheet, cover prove until doubled in size, about 30 minutes.

8 Preheat oven to 200°C / 400°F / gas mark 6

9 Press down on the top of the dough with your fingers to form dimples. Sprinkle liberally with olive oil, sea salt and fresh rosemary.

10 Bake in the preheated oven for 20 minutes or until crisp and golden. Serve straight from the oven.

ARANCIATA NUORESE
sardinian 'nougat'

This delectable sweet celebrates honey, almonds and orange peel, and it is made and used during the winter months as an energy food, a pick-me-up – it's delicious as well, of course! It's a sort of soft panforte, but not so crunchy or sticky, which can be randomly cut and served with coffee.

SERVES 8

225g (8oz) fresh unwaxed orange peel (about 4 large oranges)

225g (8oz) fragrant honey, preferably from Sardinia

225g (8oz) blanched almonds, toasted and roughly chopped

MIELE

honey is not strictly a winter ingredient, but its sticky texture and delicious sweetness make it ideal for the season's cakes, sweets and puddings. the world's oldest sweetener, made by bees from the nectar of flowers. The type of flower the nectar comes from affects both colour and flavour. Rosemary and acacia honeys, for example, are pale and delicate, whilst pine honey is dark amber with a strongly resinous flavour. Flavour is also influenced by weather and season: spring honeys are soft and sweet; summer ones are richer. The tendency of honey to crystallise depends on the natural balance of sugars it contains, thus you can find clear or runny honeys, and set or granulated honeys. Honey can be used to replace sugar in cakes, pastries and biscuits, something I enjoy doing. one of the first ways to enjoy honey other than cooking with it is to serve it with a combination of a fine cheese, preferably Pecorino, and fresh pears.

1 Before weighing the peel carefully wash your oranges in cold water to get rid of any blemishes. Use a sharp knife to remove the peel from the oranges and eliminate as much of the white part as possible.

2 Cut the peel into strips as long and thin as possible. Place the peel in a dish, fill with water, cover and store at room temperature for a day.

3 Drain the dish, then, fill with fresh water. Cover and store for another day.

4 Drain the peel completely and pat dry. Putl in a saucepan along with the honey, and heat over a moderate heat for 30 minutes. Add the toasted almonds and stir.

5 Transfer to a dampened shallow tray, and let cool. When cold, the texture is sticky and semi-soft.

ZEPPOLE

honey and spice twists

These are traditionally eaten on Christmas Eve – a huge pyramid of golden light pastries, smothered in honey and mixed spice. My grandmother used to get up early on Christmas Eve morning especially to make them. They are delicious, but take a bit of practice to make.

SERVES 4–5

1 Blend the fresh yeast with 2 tbsp of the hand-hot water. If using dried yeast, sprinkle it into 2 tbsp of the water with the pinch of sugar, and leave in a warm place for 15 minutes until frothy. Meanwhile, sift the flour and salt into a large bowl, and make a well in the centre. Pour the yeast liquid, beaten egg and some of the remaining water into the centre and mix together, gradually adding the remaining water, to form a dough.

2 Turn the dough on to a well floured surface and knead for 10 minutes until smooth. Put the dough in a lightly oiled bowl, cover with a clean tea towel and leave to rest for 20 minutes.

3 Take a chestnut-sized piece of dough and roll into a thin sausage shape, then cross the ends to form a loop at one end. Continue shaping the dough to make 15 zeppole.

4 Heat the olive oil in a saucepan. Deep-fry five pieces of dough at a time. When they bob to the surface, remove from the oil and drain on kitchen paper. When all the dough is cooked, dust the zeppole with caster sugar and the mixed spice. Pile them into a pyramid on a serving plate.

5 Heat the honey in a small saucepan, then pour over the top of the zeppole. Serve on the same day you make them.

15g (½oz) fresh yeast or 1½ teaspoon dried yeast and a pinch of caster sugar

150ml (¼ pint) hand-hot water

caster sugar for dusting

225g (8oz) plain white or Italian type 00 plain flour

a pinch of fine sea salt

1 large egg, beaten

olive oil for deep frying

2 tbsp ground mixed spice

3 tbsp clear honey

SEBACLAS
cheese biscuits with honey

This recipe could be said to be an example of Sardinian frugality. There is always some cheese around, some eggs, and some semolina (most Sardinian breads are based on semolina). To serve the crisp fried rounds with honey may seem unusual, but the combination works very well. The sweetness of the honey counters and balances the saltiness of the cheese.

SERVES 8

300g (10½oz) semolina flour or Italian 00 plain flour

1 large egg, beaten

150g (5½oz) Pecorino Sardo cheese, grated

a pinch of fine sea salt

olive oil for deep frying

fragrant clear honey

1 Mound the semolina or flour on a board and make a well in the centre.

2 Mix in the egg, cheese, salt and enough water to make a soft, elastic dough. Water quantity can vary considerably depending on the type of flour used. Tap into your instincts, adding water cautiously to enable you to get the right texture.

3 Roll the dough into cylinders and cut these into small pieces. Roll between the palms of your hands to make balls, 2.5cm (1in) in diameter. With floured hands, flatten them into very thin circles.

4 Heat the oil to 180°C /350°F / gas mark 4. Fry the rounds until they turn pale golden. Drain well on paper towels and serve with honey.

TORTA DI CIOCCOLATA AL FORNO CON VANIGLIA E NOCCIOLA

baked chocolate cheesecake with vanilla & hazelnuts

For all chocolate – cheesecake lovers – in moderation of course! This pudding has a dense, fudgy texture.

SERVES 6

115g (4oz) digestive biscuits

250g (9oz) good quality plain chocolate

200g (7oz) unsalted butter

150ml (¼ pint) soured cream

½ tsp vanilla extract

2 large eggs

125g (4½oz) caster sugar

500g (18oz) cream cheese

150ml (¼ pint) whipping cream

125g (4oz) shelled hazelnuts, chopped

To decorate:

6 shelled hazelnuts

CIOCCOLATA

chocolate appears in this winter chapter not because it is seasonal, but because it is so richly satisfying and warming. It was first brought to Spain in 1528 by Cortes, and its popularity quickly spread throughout Europe. Chocolate is made from the pods of a tropical tree, Theobroma cacao (which means 'food of the gods'). The beans and pulp in the pods are fermented, dried, then roasted. The more of the cocoa solids or butter there is in a chocolate, the more bitter, intense and better quality the chocolate will be. Use chocolate that is at least 75 per cent cocoa solids. Chocolate is not much used in Italian cooking, although there are some delicious chocolate puddings.

1 To make the crust: put the biscuits in a strong polythene bag and crush with a rolling pin. Grate 25g (1oz) of the chocolate. Melt 85g (3oz) of the butter, add the crumbs and grated chocolate, and mix the ingredients well together.

2 Press the mixture into the bottom of a 23cm (9in) spring-form cake tin.

3 To make the filling: break the remaining chocolate into a bowl and add the remaining butter. Place over a saucepan of simmering water until the mixture is smooth, stirring all the time. Stir in the soured cream and vanilla and heat gently, then remove from the heat.

4 Preheat the oven to 170°C / 325°F / gas mark 3. Put the eggs and sugar in a bowl and whisk together until the mixture is thick and pale and forms ribbons when the whisk is lifted. Beat in the cream cheese, stir in the chocolate mixture and fold in the chopped nuts.

5 Pour the filling onto the base in the cake tin and bake in the preheated oven for two hours. Leave to cool then chill in the fridge (it will sink in the centre).

6 Before serving, remove the cheesecake from the tin. Whip the cream until it stands in soft peaks then use it to decorate the cheesecake, along with the hazelnuts.

TORTA DI CIOCCOLATA
chocolate cheesecake

This pudding is for all chocolate and cheesecake lovers, and has a dense, fudgy texture. I first encountered it in Perugia, in a bar called Sandri. Because the bar was so busy, I couldn't get any details of the recipe, so I have made it up – but I think I have managed to capture the richness of that wonderful chocolate experience!

SERVES 6

400g (14oz) darkest, best chocolate available, broken into pieces

250g (9oz) unsalted butter

5 large eggs

4 tbsp dark muscovado sugar

125g (4½oz) ground almonds

125g (4½oz) Italian 00 plain flour

1 tsp baking powder

2 tsp vanilla extract

Chocolate glaze:

125ml (4fl oz) single cream

125g (4½oz) darkest, best chocolate available, chopped

To serve:

85g (3oz) mixed berries, chilled

150ml (¼ pint) double cream, whipped

1 Preheat the oven to 160°C / 325°F / gas mark 3, and grease and base line a 23cm (9in) cake tin.

2 Place the chocolate and butter in a bowl over a saucepan of simmering water, and stir until smooth. Set aside.

3 Place the eggs and sugar in a bowl and beat until light and fluffy, about six minutes. Fold in the almonds, flour, baking powder, vanilla and the chocolate mixture. Mix well.

4 Pour the mixture into the prepared cake tin and bake in the preheated oven for 45 minutes, or until the cake is cooked when tested with a skewer. Cool the cake in the tin.

5 To make the chocolate glaze: heat the cream in a saucepan until almost boiling then remove from the heat. Stir in the chocolate and continue stirring until the chocolate has melted and is smooth.

6 Spread the cake with the chocolate glaze, cut into wedges and serve with the chilled berries and cream.

BÔNET
chocolate pudding

This classic chocolate pudding from Piedmont is so-named for its bonnet-like shape. It is a recipe reputed to date from around the sixteenth century. The introduction of amaretti biscuits is more recent, possibly displaying a French influence, for Italy is not really renowned for her puddings. Cocoa is used now instead of chocolate, for convenience, and, if you use the best, for the ultimate flavour (see page 124).

SERVES 8

100g (3½oz) demerara sugar

4 large eggs

2½ tbsp unsweetened cocoa powder

250ml (9fl oz) whole milk

1 tbsp white rum

1 tbsp dry Marsala wine

45g (1½oz) amaretti biscuits, crushed

1 Preheat the oven to 130°C / 250°F / gas mark 1. Warm a 1 litre (1¾ pint) ring mould in the oven whilst making the syrup.

2 Heat 50g (1¾oz) of the sugar in a small, heavy saucepan until the sugar begins to melt around the edges of the pan. Stir with a wooden spoon until the sugar dissolves into a smooth syrup that is nutty brown. Quickly pour the syrup into the warm mould and rotate the mould to coat the entire inner surface evenly.

3 Bring a kettle of water to the boil, to use for a bain-marie. Beat the eggs in a large bowl with a wire whisk until foamy. Add the remaining sugar and continue to beat until the sugar is dissolved. Blend in the cocoa, then add the milk, rum and Marsala. Stir in the crushed amaretti and pour the mixture into the caramelised mould.

4 Cover the mould with foil and place it in a large pot. Fill the pot with enough of the boiling water to come halfway up the sides of the mould. Steam the bônet in gently simmering water for 15 minutes in the preheated oven. Remove the mould from the bain-marie; leave to cool then refrigerate.

5 30 minutes before serving, unmould the bônet on to a serving platter. Spoon any syrup that remains in the mould over the pudding.

DOLCE DI NATALE
christmas eve cake

This cake has nothing to do with chocolate, but it is a splendid recipe with which to finish the book! It is laden with good, rich, seasonal ingredients, and makes a very interesting alternative to the traditional British Christmas cake or an Italian panettone. In Italy and elsewhere in Europe, Christmas Eve is the time for major celebration. We would have this with an espresso before opening our gifts.

SERVES 8

125g (4½oz) raisins

13 dried figs, stemmed and chopped

250g (9oz) shelled fresh walnuts, lightly toasted and coarsely chopped

175g (6oz) pine kernels, toasted

1 tbsp grated unwaxed orange zest

6 tbsp grappa

300g (10½oz) Italian 00 plain flour

½ tsp baking powder

¼ tsp fine sea salt

175g (6oz) unsalted butter

125g (4½oz) golden caster sugar

4 large eggs

4 tbsp whole milk

vanilla icing sugar, to dust

1 In a bowl, cover the raisins with hot water and soak for 10 minutes. Drain and place in a bowl, along with the figs, walnuts, pine kernels and orange zest. Cover with a cloth and set aside for 30 minutes.

2 Meanwhile, preheat the oven to 190°C / 375°F / gas mark 5, and grease and line a 25cm (10in) round cake tin.

3 In another large bowl, sift together the flour, baking powder and salt.

4 In yet another medium bowl, beat the butter and sugar together until fluffy and creamy. Beat in the eggs, one at a time. Add half of the dry ingredients to the butter mixture and stir. Mix in the milk and the remaining dry ingredients. Fold in the nut mixture.

5 Transfer the batter to the prepared tin, and bake in the preheated oven for one hour. Remove from the tin and cool on a rack. Sprinkle with vanilla-flavoured icing sugar if you like.

INDEX

A

almonds 171–5, 179
anchovies 27, 33, 71, 76, 91, 102
anise and bay crown loaf 194
antipasti 102, 106
aperitif cocktail 59
apple and rosemary cake 160
artichokes *see* globe artichokes
asparagus 14
  asparagus flan 17
  omelette 15
  risotto with wild asparagus 18
aubergines 132
  stewed vegetables 134
  marinated aubergine 135
Autumn recipes 126–81

B

basil 100, 202
bay 192, 194
bay liqueur 193
beans and peas
  borlotti beans 187, 190
  broad beans 28, 86–7, 87
  cannellini beans 184, 186
  green beans 79
  peas 80
biscuits
  almond 172
  cheese biscuits with honey 216
  chocolate almond 175
  fruit and nut 179
  lemon walnut 170
  black cabbage with toasted bread and cannellini beans 184
bottarga 112
  with macaroni 114
  salad 112

bread
  anise and bay crown loaf 194
  brioche (for sweet pizza) 122
  bread salad 96
  ciabatta 206–7
  country-style 184, 186
  gnocchi 42
  Tuscan bread 208
  sweet flatbread 53
  Stromboli 92–5
  used in stuffing 111
broccoli 27, 84
bucatini with sardines 149
buffalo mozzarella 89

C

cabbage
  black cabbage 184, 186, 187
  Savoy cabbage 187
cakes
  cherry cake 119
  Christmas Eve cake 221
  hazelnut cake 181
  lemon cake 1 54
  see also cheesecake
cannelloni with broad beans and ricotta 86–7
cardoons 197
  fried with tomato sauce 197
carrots 25, 26
  roasted with sage 25
casserole, mixed seafood 115
cheese
  cheese biscuits with honey 216
  cottage cheese 55
  cream cheese 217
  Fontina 21, 154, 205
  Gorgonzola 167
  mascarpone 99, 120, 151, 162

mozzarella see buffalo mozzarella
  Parmesan 17, 18, 21, 22, 42, 68, 72, 83, 90, 92, 95, 97, 98, 131, 151, 168, 195
  pecorino 28, 86–7, 106, 165, 168, 216
  Provolone 72
  ricotta 17, 22, 52, 83, 86, 151, 171
  stracchino 155
  Taleggio 21
  see also fondue
cheesecake
  baked chocolate cheesecake with vanilla and hazelnuts 217
  chocolate cheesecake 219
  lemon cake 2 (torta di limone II) 55
  see also cake
cherries 119, 120
  cherry cake 119
  cherry tart 120
chestnuts 177–8
chicory 155, 188, 189
chillies 15, 106
chocolate 217
  baked chocolate cheesecake with vanilla and hazelnuts 217
  chocolate almond biscuits 175
  chocolate cheesecake 219
  chocolate ice-cream 124
  chocolate pudding 220
  Palermo figs and chocolate 161
  stuffed figs 162
  chocolate drink 124
Christmas recipes 215, 221

ciabatta 206–7
clams 115
cocoa 124, 220
cod, dried and salted 202
  with tomatoes and basil 202
coffee 125
  zabaglione with espresso coffee 125
courgette flowers 66
  fish wrapped in courgette flowers 49
  stuffed with mozzarella and anchovies 71
courgettes 49, 66
  baked with mint and garlic 68
  baked stuffed courgettes 69
  with vermicelli 72
crab with lemon 44

D

desserts 220
  cherry tart 120
  chestnut pudding 178
  chocolate pudding 220
  lemon cream 57
  melon sorbet 116
  sweet pizza 122
  zabaglione with espresso coffee 125
  zabaglione semi freddo 121
  see also cheesecake; ice-cream

E

Easter recipes 22, 52
eel 199
  with raisins 199
endive 188
  in mixed greens 84
  with pistachio nuts 29

F

farro 190
fennel 148
  baked fennel and
    cheese 154
  bucatini with sardines
    149
cheese and walnut salad
  165
  fennel raviolini with
    roasted vegetables
    and saffron sauce
    151–2
  Ferrigno family pasta
    155
  fried fennel 157
Ferrigno family aperitif
  59
Ferrigno family pasta
  155
figs 161
  Palermo figs and
    chocolate 161
  stuffed figs 162
fish dishes
  baked squid with
    potatoes 111
  bottarga salad 112
  crab with lemon 44
  eel with raisins 199
  fish broth 198
  fish wrapped in
    courgette flowers 49
  macaroni with
    bottarga 114
  marinated swordfish
    48
  mixed seafood
    casserole 115
  salt cod with tomatoes
    and basil 202
  spaghetti with prawns
    47
flan, asparagus 17
fondue
  fonduta Piemontese
    205
  see also cheese
fruit
  dried 179, 199

summer fruits 121, 122
see also apples;
  cherries; lemon;
  pears

G

garganelli, with spring
  vegetables 26
garlic 136, 137
globe artichokes 20
  stuffed 21
gnocchi
  bread gnocchi 42
  potato gnocchi 34–7
  Roman style 98
  semolina pizza with
    tomatoes 97
  spinach gnocchi with
    porcini mushrooms
    143
greens, mixed - sautéed
  84

H

hazelnuts 179, 181, 217
honey 214
  with cheese biscuits
    216
  in Sardinian nougat
    214
  and spice twists
    215
  in stuffed figs 162

I

ice-cream
  bitter chocolate ice-
    cream 124
  rice ice-cream 99

L

leeks 128
  leek risotto with nuts
    and vin santo 131
  in vegetable broth
    130
lemon 50
  crab with lemon 44
  Easter pie 52

lemon cake (1 & 2)
  54–5
lemon cream 57
lemon liqueur
  58, 59
lentils, with chestnuts
  177
lettuce 28
  escarole with
    pistachio nuts 29
  rocket salad with
    broad beans 28
limoncello 58, 59
liqueurs
  bay liqueur 93
  lemon liqueur 58, 59

M

macaroni
  with bottarga 114
  with fresh peas 80
marinated aubergines
  135
marinated swordfish 48
melon sorbet 116
mint 38, 43, 68
mushrooms 139
  porcini 139, 140–2,
    146, 199
mussels 115

N

nougat 214
nuts 164, 165–81

O

oakleaf lettuce 28
olive oil 187
omelettes
  asparagus 15
  wild herb 41
oregano 106
  preserved tomatoes
    with oregano 106

P

pancakes, stuffed with
  spinach and
  mozzarella 90
parsley 195

pasta dishes
  bucatini with sardines
    149
  cannelloni with broad
    beans and ricotta
    86–7
  fennel raviolini with
    roasted vegetables
    and saffron sauce
    151–2
  Ferrigno family pasta
    155
  garganelli with spring
    vegetables 26
  macaroni with fresh
    peas 80
  penne 155
  ravioli with green
    chicory 189
  rigatoni with broccoli
    27
  spaghetti with garlic
    and olive oil 137
  spaghetti with prawns
    47
  vermicelli with
    courgettes 72
pastries
  Easter pie 52
  pastry crescents with
    mozzarella and
    roasted peppers
    76–7
  torta Pasqualina
    (Easter pie) 22
pears, with Gorgonzola
  167
peas see beans and peas
peppers
  capsicums 74, 75–7
  chillies 15, 106
  peperonata alla
    campagnola 75
pesto, rocket pesto 92–5
pine kernel cream 114
pistachio nuts 29
pizza
  semolina pizza 97
  sweet pizza 122
  white pizza 212–13

polenta 142
  with porcini
    mushrooms 142
  with two sauces 145
potato 31, 75, 132, 187
  with baked squid 111
  with mushrooms 140
  potato cake 91
  potato gnocchi 34–7
  potatoes 'done
    again' 32
  Sicilian potato salad
    33
prawns 47

R
raspberries 121
rice dishes
rice ice-cream 99
rigatoni with broccoli
  27
risotto
  crisp risotto cake 39
  leek risotto with nuts
    and vin santo 131
  with wild asparagus
    18
rocket 28, 77
  rocket pesto 92–5
rosemary 160, 212, 213
apple and rosemary cake
  160

S
saffron 39

crisp risotto cake 39
roasted vegetable and
  saffron sauce 151–2
sage leaves, fried and
  stuffed 102
salads
  bottarga salad 112
  bread and mozzarella
    salad 96
  cheese and walnut
    165
  rocket salad with
    broad beans 28
  Sicilian potato salad
    33
sardines 109, 149
sauces (salsas)
  bechamela 86–7
  cherry tomato 65
  garlic 79
  mushroom 146
  roasted vegetable and
    saffron 151–2
  tomato sauce 34, 42,
    43, 65, 147, 197, 202
  walnut 168
seafood casserole 115
semolina pizza 97
shellfish see seafood
  casserole
soups and stews
  farro and bean soup
    190
  fish broth 198
  sweet and sour cream

soup 101
're-boiled' soup 186
vegetable 130, 132,
  186, 187, 195
parsley soup 195
olive press soup 187
spaghetti
  with garlic and olive
    oil 137
  with prawns 47
spinach 22, 84, 90, 143
Spring recipes 12–59
squid, baked with
  potatoes 111
stews see soups and stews
strawberries 121
  rocket pesto and
    mozzarealla loaf 92–5
Summer recipes 60–125
sweets, Sardinian nougat
  214
Swiss chard 83
  in mixed greens 84
  stuffed 83
swordfish .48
  marinated 48
  wrapped in courgette
    flowers 49

T
tarts
  Catherine's tart 171
  cherry tart 120
tomatoes 63, 75
  cherry tomatoes 33,
    65, 112, 114

with fried cardoons
  197
preserved 106
recipes 63–5, 106
tomato sauce 34, 42,
  43, 65, 147, 197, 202
truffle, white 205

V
vanilla 217
vegetable broth 130
vermicelli, with
  courgettes 72
vin santo 131

W
walnuts 131, 162, 165,
  167, 168, 170, 171, 179
Winter recipes 182–221

Z
zabaglione
  with espresso coffee
    125
  frozen 121

ACKNOWLEDGEMENTS

Many thanks to: My grandmother, for all her simply perfect recipes, always so special and so much enjoyed by myself, my sisters, my nieces and nephews etc. Mummy, for her diligent research into the poetry used in the book, but also for being so constantly wonderful. Susan Fleming, for agreeing to work with me again, and for keeping me in order. No-one works so hard and professionally, allied with such a sense of fun. Jason Lowe, for not getting cross when a 20-minute journey took 3½ hours on a balmy June Sunday afternoon. You've done it again, Jason, fabulous work. Geoff Borin, for making the book look so good, and for his calm professional approach to everything. I loved being with you in Italy. Rebecca Spry, for looking after me so well, and for so much fun during the evolution of this book. Jamie Grafton, for your constant gentle and cool reassurance, and for always waiting when I was late for meetings. Books for Cooks, for enabling me to teach, work, write and be friends with everyone, especially Rosie and Eric. Heidi Lascelles, for organising our Tuscan trip and ensuring that everything was as perfect as always. Angelo Savino, for his amazing help when we were in Conversano.